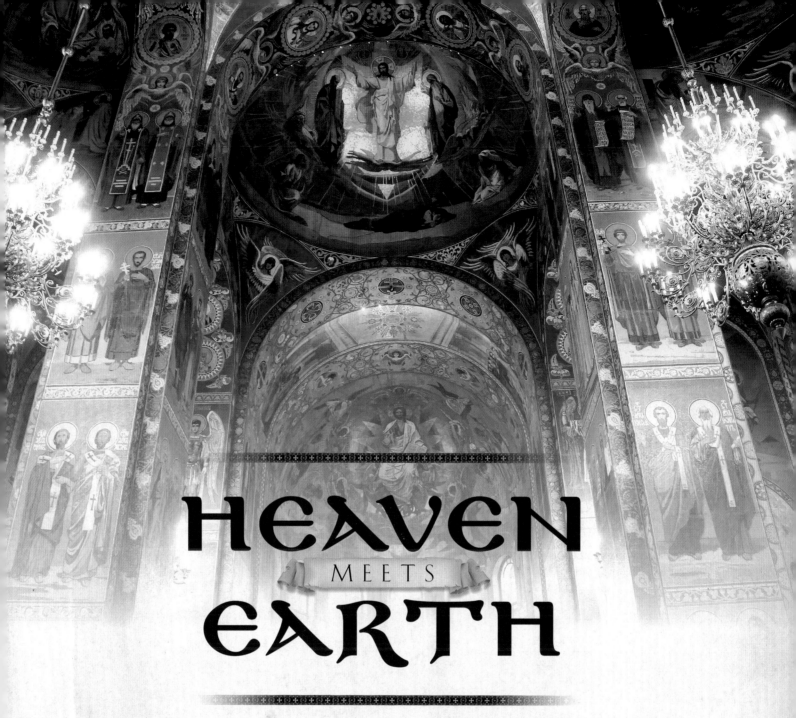

HEAVEN
MEETS
EARTH

*Celebrating Pascha and
the Twelve Feasts*

John Kosmas Skinas

ANCIENT FAITH PUBLISHING ✠ CHESTERTON, INDIANA

HEAVEN MEETS EARTH

Celebrating Pascha and the Twelve Feasts

Heaven Meets Earth: Celebrating Pascha and the Twelve Feasts
Text copyright © 2015—John Skinas

Published by:
   Ancient Faith Publishing
   A division of Ancient Faith Ministries
   PO Box 748
   Chesterton IN 46304

ISBN 978-1-936270-18-7

All Scripture quotations, unless otherwise noted, are taken from the New King James Version, © 1979, 1980, 1982 by Thomas Nelson, Inc. Used by permission.

Printed in Canada

Interior book design and cover design by Mark Wainwright of www.symbologycreative.com.

THANK YOU to Father Stephan Meholick—pastor of St. Nicholas Church in San Anselmo, California—for the sermon on August 6, 2014 (the Feast of the Transfiguration), that inspired the title of this book. All of the twelve feasts are indeed about heaven meeting earth.

—John Skinas

The editors of *Heaven Meets Earth* would like to thank: **Fathers Andrew Stephen Damick** and **Vassilios Papavassiliou** for their invaluable comments; **Valerie Yova** and **David Drillock—OCA**, for their liturgical music advice; **David DeJong** and those at **Legacy Icons**, as well as the good folks at **www.skete.com** for supplying many of the main icon images; **Ben Cabe** at BenCabe.com for his video expertise; **Istok Church Supplies** for help with the Paschal vestment fabrics; and an enormously warm thanks to the talented **Kh. Krista West**, who supplied countless vestment fabrics for background photos, and who offered her invaluable advice on festal colors and patterns.

IMAGE CREDITS:

The Nativity of the Theotokos: Main icon—available at www.legacyicons.com; icon of Joachim and Anna by Erin Kimmet of Annunciation Press at APicons.com.

The Elevation of the Cross: Photo of girl kissing cross by Niko Rakas at www.nikorakos.com.

The Entrance of the Theotokos: Illustration of Solomon's Temple taken from the *ESV® Study Bible* (*The Holy Bible, English Standard Version®*), copyright © 2008 by Crossway Bibles, a publishing ministry of Good News Publishers. Used by permission. All rights reserved.

The Nativity of Christ: Main icon—available at www.legacyicons.com.

The Theophany of Christ: Main icon—available at www.skete.com; photo of Father John Tomassi blessing the Pacific by Rdr. Michael Theophan Lujan, © 2013 Michael Lujan, photomenon.com.

The Meeting of the Lord in the Temple: Photo of baby Brigid being churched by Rebeca Groomer at www.carriedonthewind.com; nighttime photo of the cathedral in Kalamata by Andreas Tsonis; photo of candles by Kristina Roth George.

Palm Sunday: Main icon—available at www.legacyicons.com; Photo of palm crosses—Kristina Roth George.

Pascha: Main icon—available at www.legacyicons.com; Evangelists icon from www.legacyicons.com; photo of icon baskets in church by Kristina Roth George.

Holy Pentecost: Main icon—available at www.skete.com; image of choir singing Pentecost hymns at Saint Nicholas Orthodox Church, San Anselmo, CA.

The Transfiguration of Christ: Main icon—available at www.skete.com; photos of priest and fruit by Kristina Roth George.

A word about the hymns: All across the English-speaking Orthodox world, hymns are sung every day throughout the calendar year. Some of these hymns have been translated for one archdiocese directly from the Greek, and others have been translated from the Russian, and others from Arabic, etc…
This makes for quite a lovely variety of sounds and words and preferences. We knew it would be impossible to please everyone when it came to choosing the texts, so we simply did our best, trying to find wording that makes sense for the majority of today's American Orthodox faithful. Please forgive us if your favorite hymn looks a tad bit different. Don't stop singing it the way you always have! Simply use our text as a prompt and enter into the feast through song. All of the hymns listed in *Heaven Meets Earth* are translations from the Orthodox Church in America, Department of Liturgical Music and Translations. Many thanks to the OCA for sharing the fruit of their work.

TABLE OF CONTENTS

HEAVEN MEETS EARTH

Introduction

Fr. Andrew Stephen Damick

WHILE WE LIVE IN A TIME THAT IS SUSPICIOUS of narratives, lending our rhetorical trust to "fact" rather than to story, narrative is still the way we actually live our lives and make sense of our knowledge and experience. Narrative is the essential structure for all the information we process, whether in the news, in education, or in entertainment. History itself is a narrative. Even our memories are formed as narrative.

In the Orthodox Christian liturgical tradition, which was formed by the inspiration of the Holy Spirit through the work of the saints, it is precisely narrative—story and history—that we receive.

There is the Great Story of the salvation of the world by Christ, the conquering King who puts down death and inaugurates the New Covenant in His Blood. This is the Gospel—that Jesus is the Messiah, that He has risen from the dead, and that salvation has come as a result.

There are also the internal stories in Scripture that prepare the world for the New Covenant. We see the world's Creation, the fall from grace, a chosen people brought out of Egypt to the Promised Land, the giving of the Law of Moses, the exile into Babylon, the return to the land, and its conquest by foreign occupiers.

And then begins the New Covenant with the advent of Christ. He is conceived, born, and met in the temple by Simeon; He grows and is baptized. He heals, teaches, is transfigured, enters into the holy city, and is crucified. And He rises from the dead and ascends into Heaven, sitting at the right hand of the Father. And He sends the Holy Spirit to vivify the Church.

Along the way, we learn the stories found not in Scripture but in the surrounding tradition—of the birth of the Lord's mother, her entrance into the temple, and her blessed repose. And there are others.

And there are the stories of the saints, the extension of the Great Story into the lives of individual holy persons—or more properly, the incorporation of those persons into that Story. We see them do many of the same works as their Master. And they tell the story of the Gospel.

Story is what defines us as human persons. It defines the rhythms of our lives, our memories, and our identities. The Christian story is not "just" a story. It is truth, and it is truth that transforms, both in the telling and in the hearing. That is why we enter into the great feasts of the Church and build our lives around them. They are not mere commemorations but transforming stories, true in a way that is more profound than the bare search for "fact." And they determine not only our calendars and schedules but also the way we see and understand the world.

The events of the life of Christ are indeed "factual," but they are far more. Celebrating His feasts and all the feasts of the Church has the same purpose as the Scripture itself—"that you may believe that Jesus is the Christ, the Son of God, and that believing you may have life in His name."

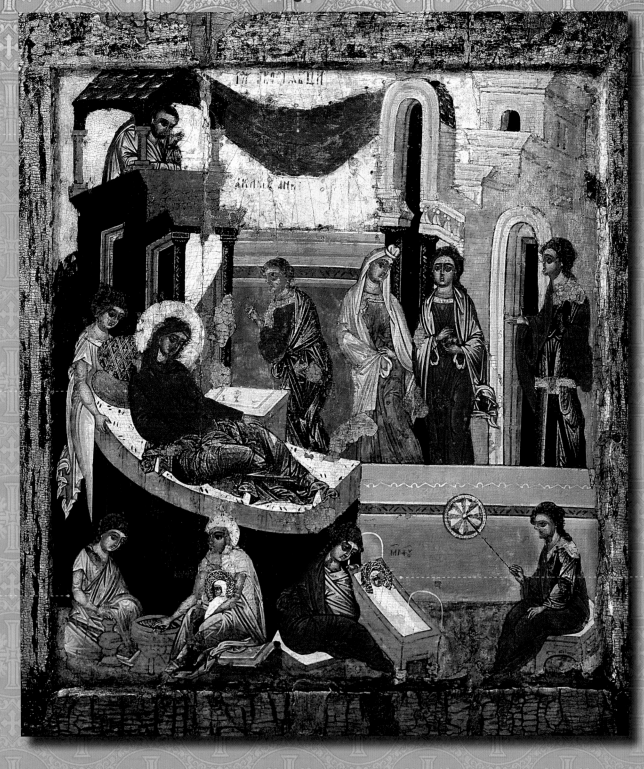

① THE THEOTOKOS, the Living Temple of God, is now in the world. Her swaddling clothes remind us of her Son's swaddling clothes, indicating that the way is now prepared for the coming of the long-awaited Messiah. The festal hymns refer to Mary as the gate through which God will come to save us.

② ANNA, whose name means "grace of God," had suffered a long time by being childless. Barrenness was humiliating and believed to be God's judgment for sin. Here, Anna reclines in wonder at God's mercy and love, her hand gesturing toward Mary, the fruit of her patience and forbearance.

③ JOACHIM, whose name means "victory of God," also gestures toward Mary, the answer to his prayers. Like Joseph in the Nativity icon, he's positioned away from the main scene. But unlike Joseph, he is not struggling with doubt; he's full of joy and wonder.

④ THE MIDWIVES bear witness to the end of Anna's childlessness, which foreshadows the coming end of the world's spiritual barrenness.

⑤ THE RED CURTAIN connecting the two buildings shows that the scene is taking place indoors. A similar curtain can be seen stretching across the tops of other "indoor" icons, such as the Annunciation and the Meeting of Christ.

THE NATIVITY OF THE THEOTOKOS
September 8

Salvation is near! The first feast of the liturgical year celebrates our new beginning. Mary, the Mother of God, is born, bringing great joy to her parents and hope to the world. It is here that the story of her Son's Incarnation and our liberation from sin and death begins, since it is in Mary that the Lord will find a place to dwell when He comes down from heaven.

Joachim and Anna were humble people who loved God and lived according to His ways. They had many material blessings and kept only a third of their wealth for themselves, giving the other two-thirds to the poor and to the temple. One blessing they lacked, however, was a child. Even though they were old, they didn't lose hope that God would grant their hearts' desire. Humiliated at the temple one day because of his lack of children, Joachim fled to the wilderness to be alone and pray. Equally heartbroken, Anna retreated to her garden and continued begging God for a child. When they reunited, both Joachim and Anna had exciting news to share. They had each been visited by an angel, who had told them Anna would give birth to a baby girl. In their overwhelming joy, they promised God they would dedicate their daughter completely to Him.

Joachim and Anna's barrenness was ended by their child, and it is their grandchild who will end the world's spiritual barrenness. Mary, the living temple in which the long-awaited Messiah would spend the first nine months of His incarnate life, was now on the earth.

Food for the Hungry

FROM THE PROTOEVANGELIUM OF JAMES*
Now her time was fulfilled, and in the ninth month Anna gave birth. She said to the midwife, "What have I borne?" The midwife said, "A girl." Then Anna said, "My soul is exalted this day," and she laid herself down.

When the required days were completed, Anna cleansed herself of the impurity of childbirth, and gave her breast to the child. She called her name Mary.

Day by day the child grew strong. When she was six months old her mother stood her on the ground to see if she could stand. Walking seven steps, she came to her mother's bosom. Her mother caught her up, saying, "As the Lord my God lives, you shall not walk on this earth until I bring you into the Temple of the Lord." Then she made a sanctuary in her bedroom, and prohibited everything common and unclean from passing through it; and she summoned the undefiled daughters of the Hebrews, and they served her.

Readings for Vespers: Genesis 28:10–17; Ezekiel 43:27—44:4; Proverbs 9:1–11

Reading for Matins: Luke 1:39–49, 56 • **Epistle Reading:** Philippians 2:5–11 • **Gospel Reading:** Luke 10:38–42; 11:27–28

*While not chosen by the Church to be part of the New Testament Canon, this book includes much of the rich knowledge about the Theotokos that was part of the Church's early life.

OLD TESTAMENT CONNECTION

From the root of Jesse and from the loins of David, Mary, the Child of God, is born unto us today, and the whole creation is made new and godlike. Rejoice together, heaven and earth: praise her, you kindreds of the nations. Joachim is glad and Anna rejoices as she cries: "The barren woman bears the Theotokos, who sustains our life." —From the Nativity of the Theotokos Matins Service

- Joachim traces his lineage to David, the messianic prophet-king of Israel.

- Anna traces her lineage to Aaron, the first high priest of Israel.

- Mary, the daughter of Joachim and Anna, is the Mother of Jesus the Messiah, the perfect fulfillment of the offices of king, prophet, and high priest.

- Abraham and Sarah: God granted them a child of promise in their old age to take away their reproach.

- Joachim and Anna: God granted them a child of promise in their old age to take away their reproach.

- Abraham and Sarah: God promises their seed will bring them descendants more numerous than the stars.

- Joachim and Anna: Through the Theotokos comes Christ, the seed whose bride is the Church, the New Israel, the countless spiritual descendants of Abraham and Sarah.

NATIVITY OF THE THEOTOKOS KATHOLIKON
RILA MONASTERY, RILA, BULGARIA

From the outside, this monastery looks like an imposing fortress, but once inside, visitors are dazzled by the cobbled courtyard, striped buildings, and rows of arches. The katholikon (main church) is adorned with vibrant frescoes and a gold-plated icon screen that took a team of woodcarvers years to complete.

FESTAL HYMNS

TROPARION: Your nativity, O Virgin, has proclaimed joy to the whole universe! The Sun of Righteousness, Christ our God, has shone from you, O Theotokos. By annulling the curse, He bestowed a blessing; by destroying death, He has granted us eternal life.

KONTAKION: By your nativity, most pure Virgin, Joachim and Anna are freed from barrenness, Adam and Eve from thecorruption of death. And we, your people, freed from the guilt of sin,celebrate and sing to you: "The barren woman gives birth to the Theotokos, the nourisher of our Life."

So by the birth of His Most Pure Mother in Nazareth He denotes sublime things. For the name "Nazareth" means a blossoming place, sacred, removed from the things of this world, adorned, as it were, with a crown, and guarded. All these epithets are clearly applicable to the Most Pure Virgin, for she is the flower sprung up from the withered tree of a barren and aged womb that has renewed our nature, which has shriveled with age. She is the flower that does not wilt, but ever blossoms with virginity. She is the most fragrant flower, giving birth to the fragrance of the only King. — St. Demetrius of Rostov

THINK ABOUT IT . . .

Joachim and Anna experienced the scorn of their world because they had no child. But through faith they persevered. They didn't despair because their prayer had gone unanswered for so long. As Christ's followers, we experience the scorn of our world. But the insults and filth society hurls at us can become spiritual soil for the seed of our faith, which is watered with patience, endurance, and humility. In this way we won't become like the barren fig tree Christ cursed, but will be bearers of the spiritual fruit (see Gal. 5:22–23) that brings beauty and nourishment to the world.

WHERE ARE YOU?

We're at the beginning of a new liturgical year; it's time for a fresh start. No matter how fruitless and dried up our spiritual lives may have become, now is the time to begin nourishing them with the feasts and sacraments of the Church. If we persevere like Joachim and Anna—staying connected to God through prayer and scripture—the parched lands of our hearts will be drenched with the living water of Christ.

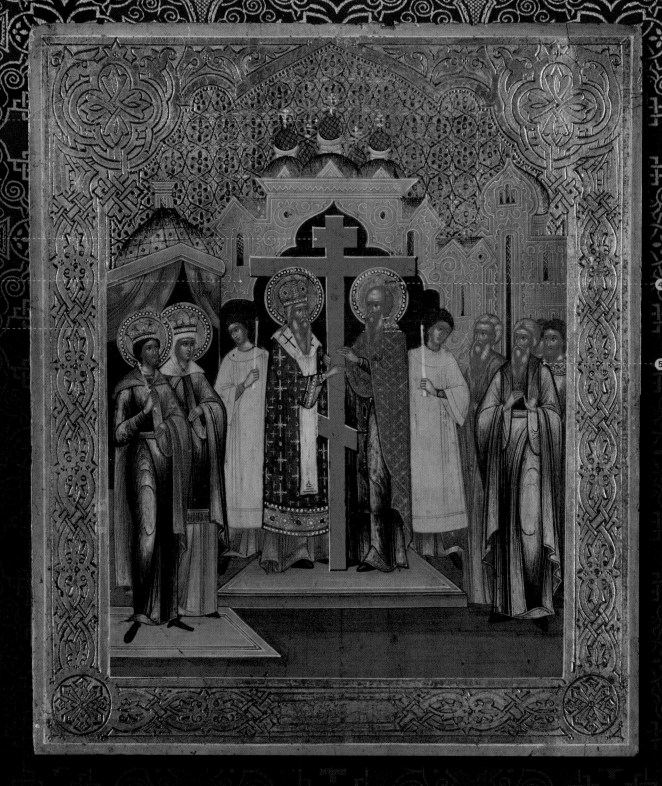

① THE CROSS raised up high for all to honor is our focus, goal, and inspiration. It is the symbol of Christ's victory over sin and death.

② SAINTS CONSTANTINE AND HELEN are prominently featured in the icon since both had profound experiences with Christ's Cross. Helen oversaw its discovery, while Constantine's miraculous vision of the Cross led to his becoming the Roman emperor and ending the persecution of Christians.

③ PATRIARCH MAKARIOS OF JERUSALEM elevates the Cross for veneration after having helped Saint Helen find it. This is the origin of the feast's and the icon's name: "The Elevation of the Precious and Life-Giving Cross."

④ EMPEROR HERACLIUS symbolizes the need to let go of earthly power and glory in order to follow Christ. He is included in the icon even though his part in the story of the Cross doesn't occur until three centuries later. Icons grant us a heavenly perspective, wherein the laws of time and space don't apply, allowing us to see people of different eras together in the same scene.

⑤ BISHOPS, NUNS, AND OTHER BELIEVERS represent the Church, the gathering of believers who take up their crosses and follow the Messiah. Christ's first disciples scattered at the sight of the Cross; now His followers gather around it.

⑥ THE CHURCH OF THE RESURRECTION depicted in the background is more popularly known as the Holy Sepulcher. The central worship space of the large complex still functions as the katholicon (main church) of the Jerusalem Patriarchate. The complex, shared by various Christian groups, includes the sites of the Crucifixion (Golgotha) and Resurrection (Christ's tomb) within its walls.

THE ELEVATION OF THE CROSS
September 14

This joyful celebration of Christ's Cross brings together various events from history, beginning with the discovery of the Cross by Saint Helen in the 300s.

When Empress Helen's subjects had found not one, but three crosses buried on Golgotha, she consulted with Makarios, the Patriarch of Jerusalem. They concluded that the Lord's Cross would be the one that would heal the sick. To everyone's joy, someone was indeed healed (or raised from the dead, according to some accounts) by being touched with the True Cross. The church held a huge celebration, during which Patriarch Makarios "elevated"—or held up—the Cross for all to venerate as they chanted, "Lord, have mercy!" This event became linked to the dedication of the Church of the Resurrection, built by Helen's son, Emperor Constantine, on the site of our Lord's tomb.

The feast also recalls the Cross's recovery from Persia by Byzantine Emperor Heraclius in the 600s. Hindered by an angelic force when he tried to bear the Cross along the route Jesus had trod, Heraclius realized that to carry Christ's Cross, he needed to remove his royal robes and walk barefoot as a lowly servant. He had to let go of power and pride in order to follow the humble way of the King of Glory.

Ultimately, this feast is a celebration of Christ's Cross as the tool of our salvation. Jesus turned the most fearsome way of death into the means of eternal life, filled with grace, power, and meaning. The height of the Cross reconnects earth with heaven, providing humanity with a way to recover from the Fall. The wood brings us back to the tree in Eden, granting us a new beginning in union with God Incarnate. The shape of the Cross points to every direction; no one is beyond the reach of its power. Through this shape, Christ stretches out His arms to embrace everyone who chooses to come to Him.

Food for the Hungry

SUNDAY AFTER THE ELEVATION OF THE HOLY CROSS, THE GOSPEL OF MARK 8:34–38; 9:1
When He had called the people to *Himself,* with His disciples also, He said to them, "Whoever desires to come after Me, let him deny himself, and take up his cross, and follow Me. For whoever desires to save his life will lose it, but whoever loses his life for My sake and the gospel's will save it. For what will it profit a man if he gains the whole world, and loses his own soul? Or what will a man give in exchange for his soul? For whoever is ashamed of Me and My words in this adulterous and sinful generation, of him the Son of Man also will be ashamed when He comes in the glory of His Father with the holy angels." And He said to them, "Assuredly, I say to you that there are some standing here who will not taste death till they see the kingdom of God present with power."

Readings for Vespers: Exodus 15:22–16:1; Proverbs 3:11–18; Isaiah 60:11–16

Reading for Matins: John 12:28–36 • **Epistle Reading:** 1 Corinthians 1:18–24 • **Gospel Reading:** John 19:6–11, 13–20, 25–28, 30–35

Additional Reading: John 3:13–17 (Sunday before the Elevation of the Holy Cross)

Symbols of the Cross in the Old Testament

■ Moses placed an image of a serpent on a wooden pole as an antidote to the venom of the snakes in the wilderness, turning the symbol of death into a symbol of life.

■ Jesus allowed Himself to be placed on a wooden cross as an antidote to the poison inflicted on the people by the devil, turning the symbol of death into a symbol of life.

■ The bitter waters of Marah were made sweet after Moses cast the wood into them.

■ The bitter waters of this life are made sweet by casting Christ's Cross into them.

■ The Tree of Life stood in the center of the Garden of Eden.

■ The Tree of the Cross stands in the center of our new spiritual paradise.

festal tradition

Basil

No matter what day of the week it falls on, this feast, unlike all the other great feasts, requires us to keep a strict fast in remembrance of our Lord's Cross. This is a powerful reminder that the feasts are about heaven meeting earth, not food meeting our stomachs. Nevertheless, many associate this feast with a well-known herb—but for its smell as opposed to its taste.

This connection comes from the story about Saint Helen searching diligently for the Cross. When she noticed the sweet smell of a plant growing on a hill outside Jerusalem, Helen asked her subjects to dig underneath the herb. It was there that she discovered the Cross. The name of the herb, basil, comes from the Greek *vasiliko*, which means "of the king." So on this feast we surround the King's Cross with basil in celebration of the abundant life that comes from it.

With reverent prostrations, priests bless the four directions with a crucifix that's been immersed in holy water. Also blessed on this day is the basil that many people bring after having grown it all summer. Priests use sprigs of this basil to sprinkle the faithful with the holy water, reminding us that we too are "of the King."

Unless a man gives himself entirely to the Cross, in a spirit of humility and self-abasement; unless he casts himself down to be trampled underfoot by all and despised, accepting injustice, contempt, and mockery; unless he undergoes all these things with joy for the  sake of the Lord, not claiming any kind of human reward whatsoever—glory or honor or earthly pleasures—he cannot become a true Christian.

—St. Mark the Ascetic

FESTAL HYMNS

TROPARION: O Lord, save Your people and bless Your inheritance. Grant victories to the Orthodox Christians over their adversaries; and by virtue of Your Cross, preserve Your habitation.

KONTAKION: As You were voluntarily raised upon the Cross for our sake, grant mercy to those who are called by Your Name, O Christ God; make all Orthodox Christians glad by Your power, granting them victories over their adversaries, by bestowing on them the invincible trophy, Your weapon of peace.

Before Your Cross we bow down in worship, O Master, and Your Holy Resurrection we glorify.

CHURCH OF THE HOLY CROSS
STAVROVOUNI MONASTERY, LARNACA, CYPRUS

The name of this monastery means "Cross Mountain." The name comes from the fourth-century account of an angel guiding Saint Helen to build a mountaintop church to house a piece of Christ's Cross. The monastery was established on the ruins of a pagan temple that had been dedicated to Zeus.

CYPRUS
LARNACA

THINK ABOUT IT . . .

To keep the Cross from being stolen again by the Persians or anyone else, the church divided it into pieces and distributed them around the world. While Christ's Cross is no longer in one piece, we still carry the whole truth of it in our hearts. Like Patriarch Makarios, we raise the cross up as our victory banner. We lift up the cross when we sign ourselves with it before meals. We lift up the cross when we endure ridicule for wearing it around our necks. We lift up the cross when we resist the very passions that nailed Christ to it.

WHERE ARE YOU?

The excitement of the new liturgical year may already be gone, and maybe we've slid back into our old sinful ways. The Church holds the Cross up to remind us of our calling. With the Cross there's nothing to fear; there's no demon that can't be conquered. Like agitated insects knocking against a pane of glass, demons can now only come into our lives if we open the window.

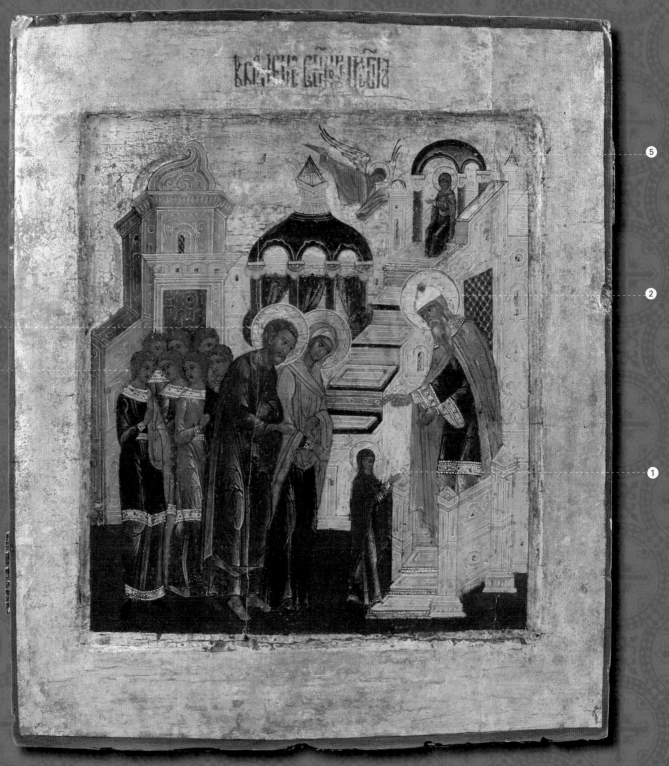

1 THE THEOTOKOS, the living Holy of Holies, rushes with outstretched arms to Zacharias at the entrance of the temple, showing the enthusiasm with which she offers herself to God. She is small but depicted with adult features and a covered head (in contrast to the young maidens) as a way of illustrating her spiritual maturity.

2 ZACHARIAS, the high priest whose name means "God has remembered," has emerged from the temple to receive and bless Mary. He senses that Israel's centuries-long wait for the Messiah will soon be over.

3 JOACHIM & ANNA, not forgetting their vow to give their long-awaited child back to God, are icons of a God-centered couple who remain lovingly faithful to Him and to each other.

4 THE YOUNG MAIDENS who escort Mary and her parents to the temple represent the Church—those who are called to "enter the King's palace" (Psalm 45:15). We learn from the festal vespers that the flames of their lamps foreshadow the Light "that is to shine forth from [Mary] and give light by the Spirit to those that sit in the darkness of ignorance."

5 THE HOLY OF HOLIES figuratively rises in the upper right corner of the scene to show that humanity is being raised back into communion with God. Having originally contained the Ark of the Covenant, it is now the dwelling of Mary, the Ark of the New Covenant. She receives bread from an angel, symbolizing her spiritual nourishment in the stone temple as she prepares to become the living temple for the incarnate God.

THE ENTRANCE OF THE THEOTOKOS
November 21

God has not only chosen Mary; she has chosen Him, fulfilling the prophecy in Psalm 45:10–11, "Listen, O daughter, consider and incline your ear; forget your own people also, and your father's house; so the King will greatly desire your beauty."

Joachim and Anna, faithful to their promise, presented their long-awaited and only child to God. Zacharias—the high priest who received Mary, and the future father of John the Baptist—played a significant role in God's plan to prepare Israel for the coming of the Messiah. He recognized Mary as the new and true Ark of the Covenant. The old ark, which was lost, had represented the spiritual presence of God among His people. Mary, the new Ark, was destined to make God physically present among His people. Recognizing this, Zacharias did the unthinkable: he brought Mary all the way into the Holy of Holies, where even he, as high priest, could only go once a year—on the Day of Atonement. Mary lived there until she was twelve, spending her childhood preparing to become the dwelling place of the Messiah as the true Holy of Holies. Her divine Child was coming to save Israel and the world by reuniting man with God. The transition from the Old Testament era to the New Testament era had begun.

Mary couldn't have been granted such divine intimacy in the Holy of Holies if she had stayed in the world. Joachim and Anna had the means to give the best of everything to Mary. They could have given her the biggest house, the greatest opportunities, or the most things. Instead they gave her God, the pearl of great price, worth so much more than all the world has to offer. Now, with the Nativity fast upon us, we are reminded that she wants to share this pearl with us.

Food for the Hungry

FROM THE PROTOEVANGELIUM OF JAMES*

When the child was three years old, Joachim said, "Let us call the undefiled daughters of the Hebrews, and let each one take a torch, and let them be burning, in order that the child not turn back and her heart be misled out of the Temple of the Lord." Thus they did, until they had gone up into the Temple.

The priest received her, and kissing her he blessed her and said, "The Lord God has magnified your name in all generations; in you, at the end of days, will the Lord God manifest his deliverance to the children of Israel." He set her on the third step of the altar, and the Lord God gave grace to her; and she danced with her feet, and all the house of Israel loved her.

Readings for Vespers: Exodus 40:1–5, 9–11, 16, 34–35; 1 Kingdoms 7:51—8:11; Ezekiel 43:27—44:4

Reading for Matins: Luke 1:39–49, 56 • **Epistle Reading:** Hebrews 9:1–7 • **Gospel Reading:** Luke 10:38–42; 11:27–28

*While not chosen by the Church to be part of the New Testament Canon, this book includes much of the rich knowledge about the Theotokos that was part of the Church's early life.

OLD TESTAMENT CONNECTION

The Ark of the Covenant

Let us praise in faith Mary the Child of God, whom long ago the assembly of prophets foretold, speaking of her as jar of manna and Aaron's rod, tablet of the Law and uncut mountain. For she is led today into the Holy of Holies, there to be brought up unto the Lord.

Matins, Exapostilarion

The Ark of the Covenant contained:

- The word of God written in stone
- Manna that came down from heaven
- The rod of Aaron that miraculously budded without water

The Theotokos, the New Ark, contained:

- The Word of God Himself in the flesh
- The Bread of Life who came down from heaven
- The Seedless Flower that sprang from the Root of Jesse

ENTRANCE OF THE THEOTOKOS KATHOLIKON IN HILANDAR MONASTERY
MOUNT ATHOS, GREECE

One of the twenty main monasteries of Mt. Athos, Hilandar was founded by St. Simeon and his son, St. Sava, the first archbishop of Serbia. The katholikon houses the famous icon "Theotokos of the Three Hands," which a divinely guided donkey carried all the way from Serbia.

MOUNT ATHOS

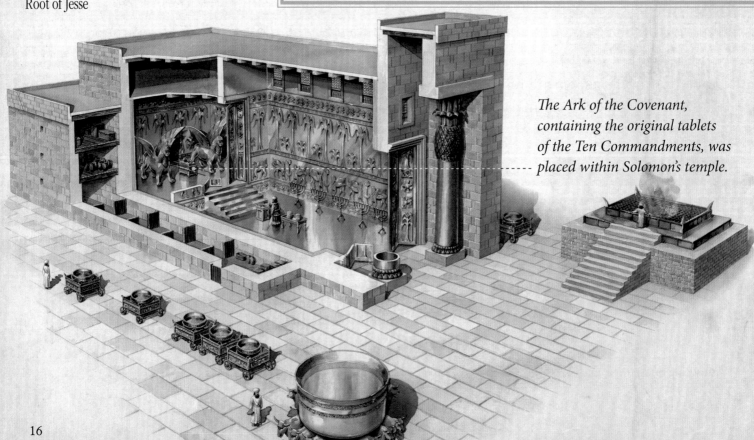

The Ark of the Covenant, containing the original tablets of the Ten Commandments, was placed within Solomon's temple.

FESTAL HYMNS

TROPARION: Today is the prelude of the good will of God, of the preaching of the salvation of mankind. The Virgin appears in the temple of God, in anticipation proclaiming Christ to all. Let us rejoice and sing to her: "Rejoice, O Fulfillment of the Creator's dispensation."

KONTAKION: The most pure Temple of the Savior; the precious Chamber and Virgin; the sacred Treasure of the glory of God is presented today to the house of the Lord. She brings with her the grace of the Spirit; therefore, the angels of God praise her: "Truly this woman is the abode of heaven."

n her manner she showed that she was not so much presented into the temple, but that she herself entered into the service of God of her own accord, as f she had wings, striving towards this sacred and ivine love. She considered it desirable and fitting hat she should enter into the temple and dwell in he Holy of Holies.

–St. Gregory Palamas

THINK ABOUT IT . . .

St. Gregory Palamas, among other Church Fathers, shows us how Mary's entry into the three sections of the temple can correspond to the three stages of our spiritual progress. (1) The court of the temple, where God's people offered sacrifice, represents purification—the first stage, during which we turn from our sinful ways and approach God's doors. (2) The Holy—the second section of the temple, where prayer was offered—is symbolic of illumination, when we begin recognizing God's handiwork all around us. (3) The Holy of Holies, where God dwelled, corresponds to theosis, when a soul is intimately united to God.

WHERE ARE YOU?

In the Gospels we're surprised by the intensity with which Christ cleanses the temple, overturning tables and chasing the merchants out with a whip. Now that Advent has begun, we're called to cleanse our very selves with the same kind of intensity. Like all holy temples, we are to be completely dedicated to the one true God. We need to rip away any images of false deities that we may have hanging over the altars in our hearts. The real One is coming.

1 JESUS THE MESSIAH is wrapped in swaddling clothes that resemble His death shroud; the manger is the same shape as His tomb; the cave of His birth resembles the cave of His burial. Church Fathers such as Ephraim the Syrian emphasize that God the Word was made flesh so that He could enter Hades and leave it powerless, freeing us from sin and death forever.

2 THE THEOTOKOS is at the heart of the icon since she is the Mother of Life, the new Eve through whom God came to reestablish the world. Her patient, understanding gaze toward Joseph, who struggles to make sense of what has happened, reassures us as we struggle with our own doubts about God and His Incarnation.

3 THE STAR receives its light from a ray emanating from the large semicircle representing God, which shines beyond the boundaries of the icon. The three rays remind us that the Son is still with the Father and the Holy Spirit in heaven after the Incarnation.

4 THE ANGELS turning toward Earth announce the good news of God's wondrous arrival.

5 SHEPHERDS, in their humility, are the first children of Israel to draw near to Christ. Some icons show a shepherd playing an instrument, joining the angels in their tuneful praise of God.

6 THE OX AND DONKEY join the Theotokos and her Child in the cave. "The ox knows his owner, and the donkey his master's crib; but Israel does not know Me, and the people have not regarded Me." (Isaiah 1:3)

7 THE MAGI, reaching Jesus later than the children of Israel, represent those who make their way to Christ from great physical, mental, or spiritual distances. The gold they bring is for the King of kings, the frankincense for the one true God, and the myrrh for His anointing after the death for which He was born.

8 JOSEPH struggles with doubt. Since the Nativity is an icon of the re-establishment of the world, the tempter—represented by the old man of worldly wisdom—is present at this new beginning. The halo reminds us that Joseph ultimately triumphed over disbelief.

9 THE MIDWIVES who bathe Jesus remind us that God truly became human with real human needs. The water itself hints at the next feast in the calendar, the Theophany, which affirms His divinity.

THE NATIVITY OF CHRIST
December 25

Christ is born! The all-powerful God enters time and space as a helpless baby to rescue us from sin and death. The Savior's mission goes beyond the expectations of His chosen people, who have been waiting for the Messiah to free them from generations of earthly hardship.

After searching for a room in crowded Bethlehem, Joseph and young Mary could only find a cave that was being used as a stable. There, among the animals, Mary gave birth to the Son of God. The busy crowds had no idea of the great event that had taken place. The humble shepherds, having been visited by an army of angels, were the only children of Israel to go see the Baby in the manger. The three wise men who followed the bright star from the East were not of the chosen people. They had been searching for truth in the lights of the heavens. Christ, the source of all truth and light, had come down from heaven for them as well. After honoring Him with gifts, they would listen to an angel's warning and take a different path back home to avoid King Herod, who didn't want anyone to threaten his earthly power.

Like the wise men, we must change our course to avoid the way of King Herod, who wanted so badly to hold onto his manner of life, no matter how terrible the cost. Despite the efforts of earthly kings, the King of the Universe is here, shining in our darkness. He was born not to create a powerful kingdom in this world, but to plant the Kingdom of Heaven in the heart of every person. The world is now changed forever. "The truth has come, the shadow has passed away" (St. Sophronios). It is the dawn of the Sun of Righteousness; let us run to the Light!

Food for the Hungry

JOHN 3:16–21

"For God so loved the world that He gave His only begotten Son, that whoever believes in Him should not perish but have everlasting life. For God did not send His Son into the world to condemn the world, but that the world through Him might be saved. He who believes in Him is not condemned; but he who does not believe is condemned already, because he has not believed in the name of the only begotten Son of God. And this is the condemnation, that the light has come into the world, and men loved darkness rather than light, because their deeds were evil. For everyone practicing evil hates the light and does not come to the light, lest his deeds should be exposed. But he who does the truth comes to the light, that his deeds may be clearly seen, that they have been done in God."

Readings for Vespers: Genesis 1:1–13; Numbers 24:2–3, 5–9, 17–18; Micah 4:6–7; 5:1–3; Isaiah 11:1–10; Baruch 3:36—4:4; Daniel 2:31–36, 44–45; Isaiah 9:6–7; 7:10–16; 8:1–4, 9–10; Hebrews 1:1–12; Luke 2:1–20

Reading for Matins: Matthew 1:18–25 • **Epistle Reading:** Galatians 4:4–7 • **Gospel Reading:** Matthew 2:1–12

festal tradition
The Christmas Tree

Three Prophecies About Christ's Birth from Isaiah

Isaiah 7:14: "Therefore the Lord Himself will give you a sign: behold, the virgin shall conceive and bear a Son, and you shall call His name Immanuel."

Isaiah 9:5–6: "For unto us a Child is born, unto us a Son is given; and the government will be upon His shoulder. His name will be called the Angel of Great Counsel, for I shall bring peace upon the rulers, peace and health by Him.

Isaiah 11:1–2: "There shall come forth a rod from the root of Jesse, and a flower shall grow out of his root. The Spirit of God shall rest upon Him, the Spirit of wisdom and understanding, the Spirit of counsel and might, the Spirit of knowledge and godliness."

STICHERON FROM VESPERS:
What shall we offer You, O Christ, who for our sakes have appeared on earth as man? Every creature made by You offers You thanks. The angels offer You a hymn; the heavens a star; the Magi, gifts; the shepherds, their wonder; the earth, its cave; the wilderness, the manger: and we offer You a Virgin Mother. O pre-eternal God, have mercy on us.

"For the tree of life blossoms forth from the virgin in the cave. Her womb is a spiritual paradise planted with the fruit divine; if we eat of it, we shall live forever and not die like Adam. Christ is coming to restore the image which He made in the beginning."

Troparion of the Forefeast of the Nativity of Christ

For the Christian, the Christmas tree is full of symbolism. It brings to mind the Tree of Life in paradise—which God, through His Incarnation, now lets us approach. The Christmas tree also reminds us of the Cross, for which He was born. It is on the Cross that He hangs as the fruit of eternal life.

The Tree of Jesse is another connection. If we look closely at Christ's family tree, we find a number of sinful people among the branches: a murderer, a harlot, a pagan. The list goes on, showing us we're not to be weighed down by the sins of our histories. Christ tirelessly beckons us to run into His wide-open arms. Through the Eucharist, the partaking of the fruit of eternal life, we all become a part of Christ's family tree, no matter how dark our pasts.

The tree encourages us to accept our royal lineage, its very shape pointing toward the Kingdom of Heaven. The star on top guides us, as the wise men were guided, into the meaning of Christmas. Little icons on the branches encourage us to offer gifts of prayer and devotion to the Christ Child. God's light, symbolized by the lights sparkling all around the tree, reaches into the deepest, darkest crevices of our being. Christ is born; let your tree glorify Him!

He was wrapped in swaddling clothes so that you may be freed from the snares of death. He came to earth so that you may reach the stars. There was no place for Him in the inn so that you may have mansions in heaven. Though rich, He became poor for your sake, so that by His poverty you might be rich.

—St. Ambrose of Milan

FESTAL HYMNS

TROPARION: Your Nativity, O Christ our God, has shone to the world the Light of wisdom! For by it, those who worshipped the stars were taught by a Star to adore You, the Sun of Righteousness, and to know You, the Orient from on High. O Lord, glory to You!

KONTAKION: Today the Virgin gives birth to the Transcendent One, and the earth offers a cave to the Unapproachable One. Angels, with shepherds, glorify Him. The wise men journey with the star, since for our sake the eternal God was born as a little child.

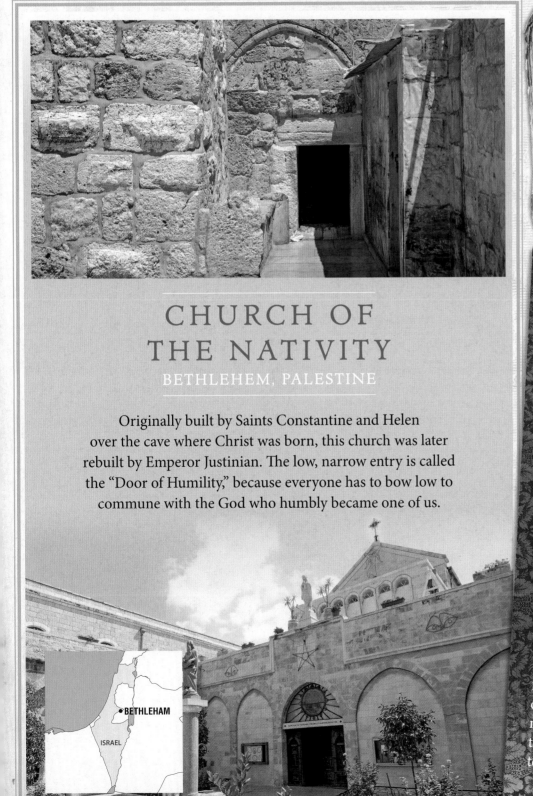

CHURCH OF THE NATIVITY

BETHLEHEM, PALESTINE

Originally built by Saints Constantine and Helen over the cave where Christ was born, this church was later rebuilt by Emperor Justinian. The low, narrow entry is called the "Door of Humility," because everyone has to bow low to commune with the God who humbly became one of us.

BETHLEHAM

ISRAEL

THINK ABOUT IT . . .

"I am the living bread that came down from heaven. If anyone eats of this bread, he will live forever."
John 6:51

For thousands of years, Israel's prophets had been waiting for this moment, the arrival of the Messiah. Yet each one of them would have been shocked that God—out of His deep, self-emptying love for us—has taken flesh and is Himself the Messiah. Equally shocking is that this God-man gives us His body for food and His blood for drink. Christ, the Bread of life, is born in Bethlehem, the "House of Bread." Laid in a feeding trough for animals, He transforms the cave into a kind of church. The manger becomes the altar where the Lamb of God offers Himself to the world.

❶ JESUS THE MESSIAH is unclothed like Adam before the Fall, signifying a new beginning for humanity and all of creation. Even as Christ bows His head before His servant John, He is blessing the water with His right hand.

❷ GOD THE FATHER & THE HOLY SPIRIT join the Son, marking this as the first full revelation of the Holy Trinity, a true Theophany, which means "appearance of God." The Father, represented by the semicircle, voices pleasure in His Son, while the Holy Spirit descends upon Christ in the form of a dove. Connected by rays of light to the semicircle, the dove occupies the same place as the guiding star in the Nativity icon.

❸ JOHN THE FORERUNNER, like the Prophet Elijah in the icon of the Transfiguration, stands at the Savior's right hand. This positioning illustrates John's fulfillment of the prophecy concerning Elijah's return to prepare the world for the Messiah.

❹ ANGELS once again bear witness to a meeting of heaven and earth. They wait in joyful wonder to receive Christ, the Incarnate God, who appears in all His glory and humility.

❺ THE JORDAN RIVER AND THE RED SEA are sometimes personified in icons by small figures in the water, as a way to connect the Theophany to the Old Testament events that prefigure the feast. A male figure represents the Jordan, which was parted and crossed by Elisha, while a female figure represents the Red Sea, through which Moses led the Israelites.

❻ THE AX AND TREE recall John the Baptist's warning that "every tree which does not bear good fruit is cut down and thrown into the fire" (Matthew 3:10).

THE THEOPHANY OF CHRIST
January 6

Heaven has opened and God has poured Himself out for us, bathing us in divine light. The Holy Trinity is revealed: Father, Son, and Holy Spirit. Jesus Christ—the Light of Light, the Second Person of this Holy Trinity—is not only among us; He has become one of us.

Saint John had been baptizing God's people with water as a sign of repentance, preparing them for the One who would baptize them with the Holy Spirit. John was taken aback when Jesus approached him for baptism, yet he obediently consented "to fulfill all righteousness." God's humility revealed His divinity, washing away man's pride and opening the gates of heaven. When Christ came out of the water, "He saw the Spirit of God descending like a dove and alighting upon Him" (Matthew 3:16). He also heard the voice of the Father, saying, "This is My beloved Son, in whom I am well pleased" (Matthew 3:17). After His baptism, Christ was led by the Holy Spirit into the wilderness to fast, pray, and prepare for the devil's temptations.

This is the beginning of Christ's public ministry; His light now begins to shine openly. The nearer we draw to His light, the more clearly we see that we're in need of repentance. God calls us to be like the Jordan itself, which tradition tells us changed direction when Christ entered its waters. Through baptism we reverse the direction of our lives, flowing away from the Dead Sea, the "sea of death" that sin leads to. When we do find ourselves sullied with spiritual dirt, we don't lose heart since, as the Church Fathers insist, one tear of repentance can be like a new baptism.

Food for the Hungry

MATTHEW 3:13–17

Then Jesus came from Galilee to John at the Jordan to be baptized by him. And John tried to prevent Him, saying, "I need to be baptized by You, and are You coming to me?"

But Jesus answered and said to him, "Permit it to be so now, for thus it is fitting for us to fulfill all righteousness." Then he allowed Him.

When He had been baptized, Jesus came up immediately from the water; and behold, the heavens were opened to Him, and He saw the Spirit of God descending like a dove and alighting upon Him. And suddenly a voice came from heaven, saying, "This is My beloved Son, in whom I am well pleased."

Readings for Vespers: Genesis 1:1–13; Exodus 14:15–18, 21–23, 27–29; 15:22—16:1; Joshua 3:7–8, 15–17; 2 Kingdoms 2:6–14; 5:9–14; Isaiah 1:16–20; Genesis 32:1–10; Exodus 2:5–10; Judges 6:36–40; 1 Kingdoms 18:30–39; 2 Kingdoms 2:19–22; Isaiah 49:8–15; 1 Corinthians 9:19–27; Luke 3:1–18

Reading for Matins: Mark 1:9–11 • **Epistle Reading:** Titus 2:11–15; 3:4–7 • **Gospel Reading:** Matthew 3:13–17

Further Reading: Luke 3:21–22; John 1:29–34

OLD TESTAMENT CONNECTION

The Flood and Baptism

When once the Divine longsuffering waited in the days of Noah, while the ark was being prepared, in which a few, that is, eight souls, were saved through water. There is also an antitype which now saves us—baptism (not the removal of the filth of the flesh, but the answer of a good conscience toward God), through the resurrection of Jesus Christ.

(1 Peter 3:20–21)

GENESIS FLOOD

- God purified the world with the waters of the Flood.
- The water brought death.
- The dove brought an olive branch to announce the end of the flood and the return of peace.
- The dove led one family out of the ark and toward land.

NEW TESTAMENT BAPTISM

- God purifies the world with the waters of Christ's Baptism.
- The water brings life.
- The Holy Spirit in the form of a dove comes upon Christ, the King of Peace.
- The Holy Spirit leads the whole world out of sin and toward heaven.

festal tradition
Blessing the Waters

The Great Blessing of the Waters takes place all around the world. In joyful continuation of Christ's act of sanctification, priests immerse a cross into a container of water three times, which recalls our Lord's three days in the grave. "We were buried with Him through baptism into death, that just as Christ was raised from the dead by the glory of the Father, even so we also should walk in newness of life" (Romans 6:4). The priests sprinkle water in every direction, blessing churches, people, and all of creation. Many church communities process to local bodies of water, blessing them as well. Through this cleansing, Christ continues making everything new.

We celebrate this newness with different traditions across the world. In warmer climates, people dive for crosses thrown into the water by bishops or priests. In the cold countries, believers carve beautiful crosses into the ice of frozen lakes or rivers; then the priests dip crosses into the "living" water beneath the surface. Some believers even immerse themselves in the icy water three times as a symbol of their baptisms. In the Holy Land, faithful have seen the Jordan reverse its flow after the blessing by the Patriarch of Jerusalem. This is also the season when priests bless the homes of the faithful, reminding us that our home life should never be separate from our church life; it all belongs to Christ, who has sanctified the waters through His Baptism for the life of the world.

FESTAL HYMNS

TROPARION: When You, O Lord, were baptized in the Jordan, the worship of the Trinity was made manifest, for the voice of the Father bore witness to You, and called You His beloved Son, and the Spirit, in the form of a dove, confirmed the truthfulness of His word. O Christ our God, You have revealed Yourself and have enlightened the world; glory to You.

KONTAKION: Today You have shone forth to the world, O Lord, and the light of Your countenance has been marked on us. Knowing You, we sing Your praises. You have come and revealed Yourself, O Unapproachable Light.

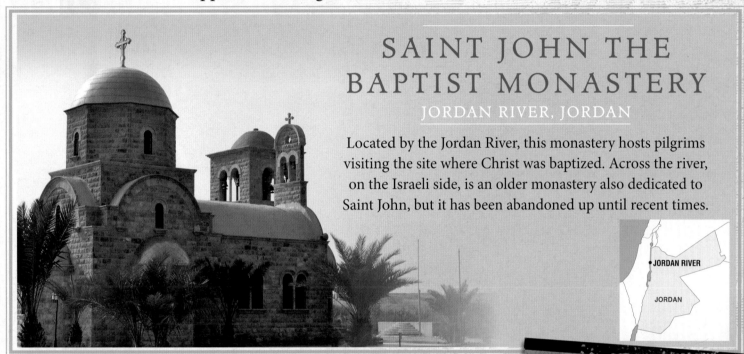

SAINT JOHN THE BAPTIST MONASTERY
JORDAN RIVER, JORDAN

Located by the Jordan River, this monastery hosts pilgrims visiting the site where Christ was baptized. Across the river, on the Israeli side, is an older monastery also dedicated to Saint John, but it has been abandoned up until recent times.

Today the waters of the Jordan are changed to healing by the presence of the Lord.
Today the whole universe is watered by mystical streams.
Today the sins of mankind are blotted out by the waters of the Jordan.
Today the darkness of the world vanishes with the appearance of our God.
Today the whole creation is lighted from on high.
Today is error annulled, and the coming of the Lord prepares for us
* a way of salvation.*
Today the celestials celebrate with the terrestrials, and the terrestrials
* commune with the celestials.*

—St. Sophronius of Jerusalem

WHERE ARE YOU?

Many people mark the beginning of a new calendar year with resolutions for self-improvement. This is also the perfect time to remember our baptisms—our new beginning with the God who has jumped into the sea of humanity to save us, the One who says, "I make all things new" (Revelation 21:5). Our sinful pasts are finished, existing no more unless we bring them back to life.

THINK ABOUT IT . . .

Theophany—like Hanukkah, the Jewish festival it's associated with—is also known as the Feast of Lights. Hanukkah celebrates the cleansing of the Jerusalem temple after pagan forces had desecrated it. Through the waters of His Baptism, Jesus now cleanses us, the temples of the Holy Spirit that had been defiled by sin. And as the oil of the Temple's menorah miraculously provided light for eight days, Christ provides us with His light for eternity. "I am the light of the world; he who follows me will not walk in darkness, but have the light of life" (John 8:12).

ΗΥΠΑ ΠΑΝΤΗ

1 JESUS THE MESSIAH, acting as our Lord and High Priest rather than a forty-day-old infant, is blessing those who have gathered around Him in the temple. Offered on our behalf, He is the spotless Lamb at the altar, which is represented by the canopy.

2 MARY THE THEOTOKOS, having just presented her Son to Simeon, extends her arms in a gesture of offering. She has given her whole being to God.

3 SIMEON THE GOD-RECEIVER recognizes this Baby as the Consolation of Israel and shows obeisance by bowing. His hands, like Mary's, are covered as a sign of reverence.

4 ANNA is identified as a prophetess by the scroll she holds. When the scroll is shown open, it often reads, "This Child made heaven and earth." Along with Simeon, Anna represents the Old Covenant, and so she is fittingly depicted pointing toward Christ.

5 JOSEPH carries the two sacrificial turtledoves. Having overcome the doubt he struggled with at the Nativity, he—like us—follows the lead of the Theotokos into deeper union with God.

6 THE TURTLEDOVES are the blood offering of poor parents who can't afford a spotless lamb for the redemption of a firstborn son. The two birds symbolize many pairings, such as Christ's humanity and divinity, the Old Testament and the New Testament, Israel and the Gentiles.

THE MEETING OF THE LORD IN THE TEMPLE
February 2

This personal encounter with the long-awaited Messiah, this meeting of heaven and earth in the temple of God, is the reason God has been keeping Simeon and Anna alive for so long. The two old prophets overflow with gratitude to God for allowing them to encounter the Christ-child.

Being pious and faithful Jews, Mary and Joseph brought Jesus to be presented to God at His temple as a firstborn son for redemption. Even though Christ was the Redeemer Himself, He had come to fulfill all aspects of the Law of Moses. Furthermore, while Mary and Joseph brought a pair of turtledoves to offer, this was ultimately unnecessary, since the babe in their arms was none other than the spotless Lamb of God who had come to take away the sins of the world. Jesus was received by the elderly and righteous Simeon, whom the Holy Spirit had led into the temple to meet the Messiah. Taking the child up in his arms, he began his famous canticle: "Lord, now You are letting Your servant depart in peace" (Luke 2:29). Simeon then prophesied about Christ being "destined for the fall and rising of many in Israel" (Luke 2:34). Anna, the elderly widow who spent all of her time fasting and praying in the temple, arrived to hear this and other prophecies about Jesus. She responded by becoming a grateful evangelist, joyfully telling everyone that the Christ had finally arrived.

According to the festal hymns, Simeon is eager to leave this world in order to share his joy with those in Hades, to tell them that the Light is coming even to their realm, bringing forgiveness and deliverance. Having received Christ on behalf of Israel, elderly Simeon, like the whole Old Covenant era, has fulfilled his purpose and is ready to pass away.

Food for the Hungry

GOSPEL: LUKE 2:22–40

Now when the days of her purification according to the law of Moses were completed, they brought Him to Jerusalem to present Him to the Lord (as it is written in the law of the Lord, "Every male who opens the womb shall be called holy to the Lord"), and to offer a sacrifice according to what is said in the law of the Lord, "A pair of turtledoves or two young pigeons." And behold, there was a man in Jerusalem whose name was Simeon, and this man was just and devout, waiting for the Consolation of Israel, and the Holy Spirit was upon him. And it had been revealed to him by the Holy Spirit that he would not see death before he had seen the Lord's Christ. So he came by the Spirit into the temple. And when the parents brought in the Child Jesus, to do for Him according to the custom of the law, he took Him up in his arms and blessed God and said, "Lord, now You are letting Your servant depart in peace, according to Your word; for my eyes have seen Your salvation which You have prepared before the face of all peoples, a light to bring revelation to the Gentiles, and the glory of Your people Israel." And Joseph and His mother marveled at those things which were spoken of Him. Then Simeon blessed them, and said to Mary His mother, "Behold, this Child is destined for the fall and rising of many in Israel, and for a sign which will be spoken against (yes, a sword will pierce through your own soul also), that the thoughts of many hearts may be revealed." Now there was one, Anna, a prophetess, the daughter of Phanuel, of the tribe of Asher. She was of a great age, and had lived with a husband seven years from her virginity; and this woman was a widow of about eighty-four years, who did not depart from the temple, but served God with fastings and prayers night and day. And coming in that instant she gave thanks to the Lord, and spoke of Him to all those who looked for redemption in Jerusalem. So when they had performed all things according to the law of the Lord, they returned to Galilee, to their own city, Nazareth. And the Child grew and became strong in spirit, filled with wisdom; and the grace of God was upon Him.

Readings for Vespers: Exodus 12:15—13:16; Leviticus 12; Numbers 8; Isaiah 6:1–12; 19:1, 3–5, 12, 16, 19–21

Reading for Matins: Luke 2:25–32 • **Epistle Reading:** Hebrews 7:7–17 • **Gospel Reading:** Luke 2:22–40

The Law of Moses

The Law of Moses is completed by the love of Christ; the honor that once belonged only to a firstborn male child of Israel now belongs to all.

OLD TESTAMENT:

Thus it came to pass, when Pharaoh was stubborn about letting us go, that the Lord killed all the firstborn in the land of Egypt, both the firstborn of man and the firstborn of cattle. Therefore I sacrifice to the Lord all males that open the womb, but all the firstborn of my sons I redeem. (Exodus 13:15–16)

NEW TESTAMENT:

For you are all sons of God through faith in Christ Jesus. For as many of you as were baptized into Christ have put on Christ. There is neither Jew nor Greek, there is neither slave nor free, there is neither male nor female; for you are all one in Christ Jesus. And if you are Christ's, then you are Abraham's seed, and heirs according to the promise. (Galatians 3:26–29)

However, brethren, we are called not only to think about this blessedness, but also to taste it in reality, for all are called to have and carry the Lord in themselves, and to disappear in Him with all the powers of their spirit. When we have reached that state, then our blessedness will be no lower than that of those who participated in the Meeting of the Lord. They were blessed who saw it; we shall be blessed who have not seen, but believed.

—St. Theophan the Recluse

festal tradition

The Blessing of Babies and Candles

Not only is this feast celebrated forty days after Christ's Nativity, it's recalled every time an infant is brought to "meet" Jesus in church for the fortieth-day blessing. In many churches, the festal hymns of Christ's Presentation are sung during the baby's presentation. This powerful tradition connects the beginning of our lives in His Church to the beginning of His life on the earth. He became one of us so that we could become one with Him. Fittingly, our presentation is our first instance of holy imitation: the priest is like Simeon, our parents are like Mary and Joseph, the people in church are joyous witnesses like Anna, and we are pure, innocent infants like the Christ-child. As the priest carries us from the narthex to the nave to the altar, he's symbolically walking us through the stages of our ever-deepening relationship with God. In many traditions, the priest raises us up like the holy gifts at the altar, consecrating our lives to God, preparing us for baptism, chrismation, and Holy Communion. We are no longer only flesh and blood; together with the other members of Christ's Church, we become transformed into part of His mystical body.

In some Orthodox churches, priests bless and distribute candles on this feast day, which is also known as Candlemas among some parishes with Western roots. Candlelight is a visible affirmation of Simeon's word about Jesus being "a light to bring revelation to the Gentiles" (Luke 2:32).

FESTAL HYMNS

TROPARION: Rejoice, O Virgin Theotokos, full of Grace! From you shone the Sun of Righteousness, Christ our God, enlightening those who sat in darkness! Rejoice and be glad, O Righteous Elder; you accepted in your arms the Redeemer of our souls, who grants us the Resurrection.

KONTAKION: By Your Nativity You sanctified the Virgin's womb and blessed Simeon's hands, O Christ God. Now You have come and saved us through love. Grant peace to all Orthodox Christians, O only Lover of Man!

PRESENTATION OF THE SAVIOR CATHEDRAL
KALAMATA, GREECE

Damaged by earthquakes and Ottoman Turks, this Byzantine-style cathedral has been rebuilt throughout its history, showing us that it's never too late to step back from destruction and reconsecrate ourselves to God. It houses a miraculous seventh-century icon of the Theotokos, through which God saved Kalamata from a plague in 1841.

KALAMATA

Christ the coal of fire, whom Isaiah foresaw, now rests in the arms of the Theotokos as in a pair of tongs, and He is given to the Elder. In fear and joy Simeon held the Master in his arms and asked for his release from life, singing the praises of the Mother of God.

—Aposticha at Small Vespers

THINK ABOUT IT . . .

*My soul hopes in the Lord,
From the morning watch until night;
From the morning watch until night,
Let Israel hope in the Lord.
(Psalm 129:6)*

In preparing to meet Christ, Simeon and Anna stayed connected to the temple, to scripture, to God. They knew this meeting was the reason God continued to give them breath for so long. Every Sunday we meet Christ more intimately than Simeon and Anna could have imagined: in the Eucharist. God grants us time to prepare for this meeting, to repent and cultivate our desire to be one with Him. Nothing in the world can eclipse this union with God. Appropriately, Simeon's famous words are used not only at the end of the day, but also after Holy Communion. Having united with Christ, we can "depart in peace" to wherever God calls us to go.

WHERE ARE YOU?

We now begin moving away from the winter feasts that celebrate the arrival of the purifying Light, and we begin looking toward Lent, the spiritual springtime in which our souls will be nourished by prayer, scripture, and liturgical services. We are called to think of what we need to move out of the way so more of the Light can shine into our lives.

29

1 JESUS THE MESSIAH is here, even though we can't see Him. He's in the Theotokos's womb, as fully human as He is at the Nativity or any other point in His life. This is His Incarnation.

2 MARY is shown sitting on a throne since she is "more honorable than the cherubim and more glorious beyond compare than the seraphim." She herself has become the throne of God. The yarn in her left hand shows that just as (according to tradition) she's stitching together the veil of the temple, the incarnate God now begins to be "stitched together" in her womb. Her raised right hand indicates both her acceptance of God's plan and a prudent hesitancy at the angel's words.

3 THE ARCHANGEL GABRIEL rushes toward Mary, feet far apart and one wing blowing back to show the urgency of his message. The other wing is raised toward heaven. In his left hand he holds the staff of a messenger, while his right hand is extended to show that he is bringing Mary the good news. Gabriel, whose name means "God is mighty," reveals that the Mighty One will make Himself helpless for us.

4 GOD THE FATHER & THE HOLY SPIRIT, as in other festal icons, are represented by the semicircle at the top of the icon. The hue is dark, showing it is the unknowable God who will be carried in Mary's womb. The ray that reaches all the way down to Mary represents the descent of the Holy Spirit.

THE ANNUNCIATION
March 25

Bearing a message from heaven, the angel rushes toward Mary. After a moment of humble hesitation, she accepts God's plan, and the world is changed forever. Now "all generations will call [her] blessed" (Luke 1:48).

The time had come for God to announce to His people the good news, which is what the name of this feast means. But before going to Mary, the angelic messenger appeared to Zacharias, the high priest who had received her into the temple when she was three years old. The archangel Gabriel revealed to Zacharias that his role in God's plan was not finished. Elizabeth, his barren wife, would conceive a child whose name would be John. This child would become a messenger like Gabriel, sent to prepare God's people for the Son of God. It was after this announcement that the angel appeared to Mary, Elizabeth's teenaged relative. Gabriel called her "highly favored" and "blessed." In her humility, Mary was troubled at being called such things. But Gabriel reassured her, saying that she had "found favor with God," that through "the power of the Highest" she would be the one to give birth to His Son. Mary responded with God-pleasing obedience: "Behold the maidservant of the Lord! Let it be to me according to your word" (Luke 1:38). This was the good news: Through Mary's cooperation, God was going to save us by becoming one of us.

Immediately after the Annunciation, Mary "entered the house of Zacharias and greeted Elizabeth," who met her with the words, "Blessed are you among women, and blessed is the fruit of your womb" (Luke 1:40–41). Not only did Elizabeth learn through the Holy Spirit that Mary was the mother of the Lord, but even John the Baptist leaped for joy in her womb. It's time for all of us to rejoice and prepare—God is now with us!

Food for the Hungry

LUKE 1:24–38

Now after those days his wife Elizabeth conceived; and she hid herself five months, saying, "Thus the Lord has dealt with me, in the days when He looked on me, to take away my reproach among people."

Now in the sixth month the angel Gabriel was sent by God to a city of Galilee named Nazareth, to a virgin betrothed to a man whose name was Joseph, of the house of David. The virgin's name was Mary. And having come in, the angel said to her, "Rejoice, highly favored one, the Lord is with you; blessed are you among women!"

But when she saw him, she was troubled at his saying, and considered what manner of greeting this was. Then the angel said to her, "Do not be afraid, Mary, for you have found favor with God. And behold, you will conceive in your womb and bring forth a Son, and shall call His name Jesus. He will be great, and will be called the Son of the Highest; and the Lord God will give Him he throne of His father David. And He will reign over the house of Jacob forever, and of His kingdom there will be no end."

continued on page 32

continued from page 31

Then Mary said to the angel, "How can this be, since I do not know a man?"

And the angel answered and said to her, "The Holy Spirit will come upon you, and the power of the Highest will overshadow you; therefore, also, that Holy One who is to be born will be called the Son of God. Now indeed, Elizabeth your relative has also conceived a son in her old age; and this is now the sixth month for her who was called barren. For with God nothing will be impossible."

Then Mary said, "Behold the maidservant of the Lord! Let it be to me according to your word." And the angel departed from her.

Readings for Vespers: Genesis 28:10–17; Ezekiel 43:27—44:4; Proverbs 9:1–11

Reading for Matins: Luke 1:39–49, 56
Epistle Reading: Hebrews 2:11–18
Gospel Reading: Luke 1:24–38

SIMILARITIES BETWEEN HANNAH'S PRAYER

(Her response to God for allowing her to conceive despite being barren)

& THE MAGNIFICAT

(Mary's response to God for allowing her to conceive despite being a virgin)

Note: Mary's conception by the barren Anna is celebrated on December 9, which is also the feast day of Hannah. Also barren, Hannah conceived Samuel, an Old Testament type of Christ. As a faithful Jew, the Theotokos very likely had Hannah's prayer memorized and in mind when she prayed the Magnificat in Zacharias's house after the Annunciation.

HANNAH'S PRAYER	MARY'S MAGNIFICAT
My heart is strengthened in the Lord; my horn is exalted in my God (1 Kingdoms 2:1)	My soul magnifies the Lord (Luke 1:46)
I rejoice in Your salvation (1 Kingdoms 2:1)	And my spirit has rejoiced in God my Savior (Luke 1:46–48)
Because no one is holy like the Lord, no one is righteous like our God (1 Kingdoms 2:2)	For He who is mighty has done great things for me, and holy is His name (Luke 1:49)
He raises the poor from the earth and lifts the needy from the dung heap (1 Kingdoms 2:8)	He has put down the mighty from their thrones, and exalted the lowly (Luke 1:52)
Those who were full of bread were made empty, and the hungry have forsaken the land (1 Kingdoms 2:5)	He has filled the hungry with good things, and the rich He has sent away empty (Luke 1:53)
He gives strength to our leaders (1 Kingdoms 2:10)	He has helped His servant Israel (Luke 1:54)

In the days of the creation of the world, when God was uttering His living and mighty "let there be," the word of the Creator brought creatures into the world. But on that day, unprecedented in the history of the world, when Mary uttered her brief and obedient, "so be it," I hardly dare say what happened then—the word of the creature brought the Creator into the world.

—Saint Philaret of Moscow

FESTAL HYMNS

TROPARION: Today is the beginning of our salvation, the revelation of the eternal mystery! The Son of God becomes the Son of the Virgin as Gabriel announces the coming of Grace. Together with him let us cry to the Theotokos: Rejoice, O full of Grace, the Lord is with you!

KONTAKION: O victorious leader of the triumphant hosts! We your servants, delivered from evil, sing our grateful thanks to you, O Theotokos. As you possess invincible might, set us free from every calamity so that we may sing: Rejoice, O unwedded Bride!

ANNUNCIATION KATHOLIKON IN MOLDOVITA MONASTERY
BUCOVINA, ROMANIA

Like many other monastery churches in the Bucovina region, the Annunciation's exterior walls are adorned with stunning frescoes. Also noteworthy are the tall arches of its open exonarthex. Built as a barrier against the invading Ottoman Turks, the monastery is surrounded by towers and thick walls.

THINK ABOUT IT . . .

"But will God indeed dwell with men on earth? If the heaven and the heaven of heaven will not be sufficient for You, how much less even this temple I built in Your name?" 3 Kingdoms 8:25

Christ spends His first nine months of human existence being nourished by Mary's body, making it "more spacious than the heavens" by His very presence. At the same time, He nourishes her with His own immaculate Body and Blood. Mary lives in constant, unbroken communion with God. Jesus comes into the world to take form in each one of us as well. In an ongoing miracle that can never be taken for granted, He comes into us through the Eucharist. He calls us, and we walk the spiritual path that leads to Communion at the royal gates of His holy altar, which are often adorned with icons of the Annunciation.

WHERE ARE YOU?

Just as the Lord did not force the Virgin to accept His invitation to become the Mother of God, neither does the Lord force us to accept His invitation to become sons and daughters of His Heavenly Father. Pascha, the season of victory, the springtime of the universe, is coming. Let us freely choose the way of life.

❶ JESUS THE MESSIAH enters Jerusalem with His right hand raised in blessing of the city that will crucify Him. The scroll in His left hand, showing that He is the fulfillment of the Old Testament prophecies, represents His authority and wisdom.

❷ THE CHILDREN are depicted as the ones cutting palm branches to spread on the road along with clothing to honor Jesus. Having no ulterior motives or earthly ambitions, they symbolize the pure in heart who will see God in His Kingdom.

❸ THE APOSTLES follow Jesus so that they "may die with Him" (John 11:16). Nevertheless, Jesus finds it necessary to look back and remind them that there is no other way, that in order to rise to heaven we must first lay down our lives for Him and each other.

❹ THE CROWD has gathered in Jerusalem for Passover to celebrate Israel's liberation from the Egyptians. Now they honor Jesus as the one they hope will liberate them from the Romans.

❺ THE YOUNG DONKEY, considered to be an unclean animal by the Jews, represents the Gentile nations that will carry Christ in their hearts after His work on earth is completed.

❻ THE MOUNT OF OLIVES on the left is the place Jesus rode down from on the donkey. It represents the dwelling place of God.

❼ THE BUILDINGS of Jerusalem on the right represent the dwelling place of man. Christ sheds tears for Jerusalem because, after He establishes His heavenly Kingdom, the unfaithful earthly city will fall.

❽ THE PALM TREE between the mountain and the city represents the Cross, through which the victorious Christ will bridge the gulf between man and God.

THE TRIUMPHAL ENTRY INTO JERUSALEM

Jesus receives a hero's welcome as He rides into Jerusalem. But the fact that He's riding a young donkey and not a war horse or chariot is a sign that He's a hero the people have not been expecting.

Following Christ's command, two of His disciples entered the village opposite Bethphage and found a tethered donkey, just as He had foretold. They untied the animal and brought it to Jesus, spreading their clothing on its back, for Him to ride into Jerusalem. The Passover crowd shouted "Hosanna," meaning "Save now!" Oppressed for so long, the Jewish people hoped this man with the power to bring the rotting corpse of Lazarus back to life would overthrow the Romans and reward them for generations of suffering. So they honored Him by covering the road with palm branches, the ancient symbol of joy and victory reserved for conquerors and heroes. Yet Jesus, in contrast to the Romans, entered Jerusalem not in a show of strength but in a show of humility. Unaffected by the praise, He had arrived to fully live out His earlier words: "Whoever of you desires to be first shall be slave of all. For even the Son of Man did not come to be served, but to serve, and to give His life a ransom for many" (Mark 10:44–45).

Jesus has indeed come to rescue the Jews from their oppressors—not by immediately destroying the Romans, but by eventually offering salvation to Jew and Gentile alike. As a contrast to the adults, the Church holds up children as symbols of pure and joyful faith—faith without political or personal agendas. Christ calls each one of us to "receive the kingdom of God as a little child" (Mark 10:15–16).

Food for the Hungry

JOHN 12:1–18

Then, six days before the Passover, Jesus came to Bethany, where Lazarus was who had been dead, whom He had raised from the dead. There they made Him a supper; and Martha served, but Lazarus was one of those who sat at the table with Him. Then Mary took a pound of very costly oil of spikenard, anointed the feet of Jesus, and wiped His feet with her hair. And the house was filled with the fragrance of the oil.

But one of His disciples, Judas Iscariot, Simon's son, who would betray Him, said, "Why was this fragrant oil not sold for three hundred denarii and given to the poor?" This he said, not that he cared for the poor, but because he was a thief, and had the money box; and he used to take what was put in it.

But Jesus said, "Let her alone; she has kept this for the day of My burial. For the poor you have with you always, but Me you do not have always."

Now a great many of the Jews knew that He was there; and they came, not for Jesus' sake only, but that they might also see Lazarus, whom He had raised from the dead. But the chief priests plotted to put Lazarus to death also, because on account of him many of the Jews went away and believed in Jesus.

continued on page 36

continued from page 35

The next day a great multitude that had come to the feast, when they heard that Jesus was coming to Jerusalem, took branches of palm trees and went out to meet Him, and cried out:

"Hosanna!
'Blessed is He who comes in
the name of the Lord!'
The King of Israel!"

Then Jesus, when He had found a young donkey, sat on it; as it is written:

"Fear not, daughter of Zion;
Behold, your King is coming,
Sitting on a donkey's colt."

His disciples did not understand these things at first; but when Jesus was glorified, then they remembered that these things were written about Him and that they had done these things to Him.

Therefore the people, who were with Him when He called Lazarus out of his tomb and raised him from the dead, bore witness. For this reason the people also met Him, because they heard that He had done this sign.

Readings for Vespers: Genesis 49:1–2, 8–12; Zephaniah 3:14–19; Zechariah 9:9–15

Reading for Matins: Matthew 21:1–17
Epistle Reading: Philippians 4:4–9
Gospel Reading: John 12:1–18
Additional Reading: Mark 11:1–10;
Luke 19:28–44

Hosannah!

Jerusalem was crowded with visiting Jews who had come to celebrate Passover (Pascha in Greek), the commemoration of their deliverance from slavery and death in Egypt. Little did they know that this man whom they hailed as their deliverer from slavery to the Romans was entering the city as the Passover lamb being led to slaughter. This sacrifice will release them from their slavery to sin and the eternal death that results from it. The events of Palm Sunday were spoken of long in advance, as far back as the Book of Genesis.

- "Binding his colt to a vine, and his donkey's colt to its branch, he will wash his garments in wine, and his clothes in the blood of grapes" (Genesis 49:11).

- "O Lord, save us now; O Lord, prosper us now. Blessed is he who comes in the name of the Lord" (Psalm 117:25–26).

- "Rejoice greatly, O daughter of Zion! Proclaim it aloud, O daughter of Jerusalem! Behold, your King comes to you; He is righteous and saving; He is gentle and mounted upon a donkey, even a young foal" (Zechariah 9:9).

festal tradition

Donkeys & Palm Branches

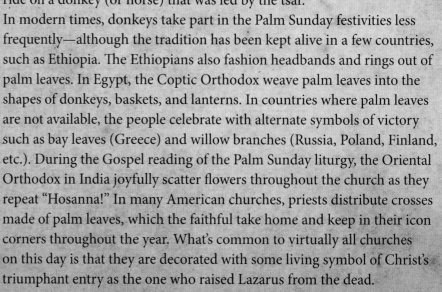

Various Palm Sunday traditions have evolved over time. In the 300s the Christians of Jerusalem followed Christ's path, waving palm leaves as the patriarch of the city followed behind on a donkey. In Constantinople, the emperor would process from his palace to Hagia Sophia in regal splendor, representing the glory of Christ the King. From the 1500s to the 1600s, the Patriarch of Moscow would ride on a donkey (or horse) that was led by the tsar. In modern times, donkeys take part in the Palm Sunday festivities less frequently—although the tradition has been kept alive in a few countries, such as Ethiopia. The Ethiopians also fashion headbands and rings out of palm leaves. In Egypt, the Coptic Orthodox weave palm leaves into the shapes of donkeys, baskets, and lanterns. In countries where palm leaves are not available, the people celebrate with alternate symbols of victory such as bay leaves (Greece) and willow branches (Russia, Poland, Finland, etc.). During the Gospel reading of the Palm Sunday liturgy, the Oriental Orthodox in India joyfully scatter flowers throughout the church as they repeat "Hosanna!" In many American churches, priests distribute crosses made of palm leaves, which the faithful take home and keep in their icon corners throughout the year. What's common to virtually all churches on this day is that they are decorated with some living symbol of Christ's triumphant entry as the one who raised Lazarus from the dead.

FESTAL HYMNS

TROPARION: By raising Lazarus from the dead before Your passion, You confirmed the universal resurrection, O Christ God! Like the children with the palms of victory, we cry out to You, O Vanquisher of death: Hosanna in the highest! Blessed is He that comes in the name of the Lord!

KONTAKION: Sitting on Your throne in heaven, carried on a foal on earth, O Christ God, accept the praise of angels and songs of children who sing: Blessed is He that comes to recall Adam.

CONVENT OF MARY MAGDALENE
JERUSALEM, ISRAEL

JERUSALEM

ISRAEL

One of the most recognizable landmarks in Jerusalem, this convent stands by "Palm Sunday Road," so called since it traces Christ's journey on the donkey from Bethphage down the Mount of Olives and up into Jerusalem. The church houses the relics of Saints Elizabeth and Barbara, the New Martyrs.

THINK ABOUT IT . . .

As Jesus begins His journey on the road to the Cross, it becomes apparent that most people don't want the kind of salvation He brings. He doesn't conform to their expectations. Today's world doesn't want Jesus' kind of salvation either. Yet like those who spread their garments before the hooves of Christ's donkey, we are called to shed our old selves and lay them in the path that Jesus takes through our lives. We can do no less than throw open the gates of our hearts. The Conqueror of Death—and everything that leads to it—is coming.

[Christ fulfills the prophecy in Zechariah 9:9] in a spiritual sense by sitting upon the donkey, the burdened Jews, and also upon the foal, the Gentiles who were coltish, untamed and unruly. For the donkey and the colt had been tethered by the reins of their own sin. Two were sent to loose them, Paul to the Gentiles, and Peter . . . to the Jews. And even now, there are two that loose us from our sins, the Epistles and the Gospel. Christ comes meekly, for He did not come to judge the world at the first coming, but to save.

—Blessed Theophylact of Ochrid

ⒷⒶⓃⒶⓉⒶⒸⒾⒸ

ⒾⒸ ⓍⒸ

❶ JESUS THE MESSIAH descends in spirit to Hades not as a victim of death, but as the victor over death. Standing on the broken doors of the underworld, Christ arrives to offer the imprisoned souls His triumph since His divine presence leads to the destruction of their bonds.

❷ ADAM AND EVE symbolize the whole of humanity. The first people to have been fashioned by the hands of Christ, they are now the first people to be lifted out of Hades by the hands of Christ. Jesus pulls them up by their wrists, emphasizing that humble surrender to Him is the most powerful action we can take for our salvation.

❸ JOHN THE FORERUNNER, representing all of the prophets, is present as the one who has prepared humanity—even the souls in Hades—to hear the good news of Christ. Gesturing toward the Savior, he occupies a position similar to the one in the icon of the Theophany.

❹ ABEL, the young shepherd son of Adam and Eve and the first innocent victim of sin and death, has been in Hades longer than anyone else. He stands as a witness to his parents being lifted back up into communion with God.

❺ KINGS DAVID AND SOLOMON, though flawed and sinful, are part of the royal line through which Christ came to establish the divine kingship that will never be corrupted by time or sin.

❻ THE SOULS IN HADES are drawn to Christ's light—symbolized by His radiant mandorla. This group often includes disciples who are still alive during Christ's descent into Hades, showing that His ultimate act of divine love goes beyond time and space. This spiritual resurrection is a foreshadowing of the physical resurrection that will take place at Christ's second coming. The risen Christ is the first-fruit of this coming resurrection.

❼ THE TWO PEAKS resemble those in the Theophany icon, between which the Jordan's waters flow. It was at the Jordan where the cleansing and illumination of creation began. Christ now floods the underworld with His light.

❽ HADES, personified by the bound figure beneath Christ's feet, is vanquished. Its chains, locks, and tools of pain lie scattered and useless. Only those who freely turn their backs on Christ's light remain trapped in the ruins of Hades.

PASCHA: THE RESURRECTION OF CHRIST

Pascha allows us to participate in the greatest event in history: Christ's Resurrection. He rises as "the firstborn from the dead" (Rev. 1:5) to rescue us from sin and death.

While Christ's Body lay in the Tomb, while His friends mourned the loss of their Teacher, something amazing was happening. In the dark realm of the dead a Light appeared, and hope was kindled among the souls that had been imprisoned since the time of Adam and Eve. This Light was the soul of Jesus, and Hades was powerless to contain it. The first rays of the Resurrection that began shining on the dead soon reached the living. On the first day of the week, as the myrrh-bearing women approached Christ's Tomb at sunrise, the earth quaked and an angel came down from heaven. Having rolled the stone away from the Tomb's entrance, he sat on it and said to them, "He is not here; for He is risen" (Matt. 28:6). There was no dead body for the women to anoint. Christ had indeed risen, leaving behind burial linens and shining angels, who told them to go spread the good news to the apostles.

This is a new beginning for all of creation. The Paschal Gospel reading from John emphasizes this by opening with the same three words that begin the Bible: "In the beginning was the Word, and the Word was with God, and the Word was God" (John 1:1). Christ, the Word of God, is He for whom creation has been yearning since the Fall of Adam. As the risen Jesus explained to His apostles, the prophecies in the Old Testament are all about Him. Now sin and death no longer have a hold on us if we allow Christ to descend into the tombs of our hearts. The death that came to us through Adam is now conquered by the life that comes to us through Christ. "For as in Adam all die, even so in Christ all shall be made alive" (1 Cor. 15:22).

Food for the Hungry

MATTHEW 28:1–20

Now after the Sabbath, as the first day of the week began to dawn, Mary Magdalene and the other Mary came to see the tomb. And behold, there was a great earthquake; for an angel of the Lord descended from heaven, and came and rolled back the stone from the door, and sat on it. His countenance was like lightning, and his clothing as white as snow. And the guards shook for fear of him, and became like dead men.

But the angel answered and said to the women, "Do not be afraid, for I know that you seek Jesus who was crucified. He is not here; for He is risen, as He said. Come, see the place where the Lord lay. And go quickly and tell His disciples that He is risen from the dead, and indeed He is going before you into Galilee; there you will see Him. Behold, I have told you."

So they went out quickly from the tomb with fear and great joy, and ran to bring His disciples word.

And as they went to tell His disciples, behold, Jesus met them, saying, "Rejoice!" So they came and held Him by the feet and worshiped Him. Then Jesus said to them, "Do not be afraid. Go and tell My brethren to go to Galilee, and there they will see Me."

Now while they were going, behold, some of the guard came into the city and reported to the chief priests all the things that had happened. When they had assembled with the elders and consulted together, they gave a large sum of money to the soldiers, saying, "Tell them, 'His disciples came at night and stole Him away while we slept.' And if this comes to the governor's ears, we will appease him and make you secure." So they took the money and did as they were instructed; and this saying is commonly reported among the Jews until this day.

Then the eleven disciples went away into Galilee, to the mountain which Jesus had appointed for them. When they saw Him, they worshiped Him; but some doubted.

And Jesus came and spoke to them, saying, "All authority has been given to Me in heaven and on earth. Go therefore and make disciples of all the nations, baptizing them in the name of the Father and of the Son and of the Holy Spirit, teaching them to observe all things that I have commanded you; and lo, I am with you always, even to the end of the age." Amen.

HOLY SATURDAY
Readings for Vespers: Genesis 1:1–13; Isaiah 60:1–16; Exodus 12:1–12; The Book of Jonah; Joshua 5:10–15; Exodus 13:20—15:19; Zephaniah 3:8–15; 1 Kingdoms 17:8–24; Isaiah 61:10—62:5; Genesis 22:1–18; Isaiah 61:1–10; 2 Kingdoms 4:8–37; Isaiah 63:11—64:5; Jeremiah 31:31–34; Daniel 3:1–90

Divine Liturgy of St. Basil: Epistle: Romans 6:3–11 • **Gospel Reading:** Matthew 28:1–20

PASCHA
Matins: Mark 16:1–8 • Divine Liturgy of St. John Chrysostom: **Epistle:** Acts 1:1–8 • **Gospel:** John 1:1–17

CHURCH OF THE RESURRECTION
JERUSALEM, ISRAEL

Across from the nave of this church—regarded as the most significant in the world—stands the actual Sepulcher (burial place) of Jesus. Every year at Pascha, a flame rises miraculously out of His Tomb and lights the candles of the Patriarch of Jerusalem, who then shares the light with the faithful.

JERUSALEM

ISRAEL

festal tradition

Eggs

From baskets loaded with delicacies to fireworks battles between neighboring churches, there are many interesting traditions around the world associated with Pascha. However, the undisputed king of Paschal tradition remains the humble egg.

MARY MAGDALENE

The story of the egg goes back to St. Mary Magdalene, one of the myrrh-bearing women who discovered Christ's empty Tomb. Having become an evangelist, she traveled to Rome to speak of Christ's Resurrection to Emperor Tiberius. One version of the story says she gave him an egg, which God—to prove the truth of Mary's words—is said to have turned as red as His saving Blood. Since then, believers have been painting eggs not only red, but other life-affirming colors as well.

PYSANKY

In Ukraine, among other countries, intricate egg painting has been raised to an art form. The painted eggs are called *pysanky*. Using beeswax and layers of dye, believers decorate eggs with designs that are rich in symbolism: ladders for prayer, fish and crosses for Christ, pine needles for eternal life, butterflies for the Resurrection, grapes and wheat for Holy Communion, the sun and stars for the light and love of God, triangles for the Holy Trinity, and on and on. Each color also carries meaning: white for purity, green for life, yellow for light, black for eternity, blue for the heavens, red for Christ's sacrificial love, gold for wisdom, and so on. Pysanky are blessed and kept in people's homes as reminders of the risen Christ's presence.

EGG-TAPPING

Egg-tapping is the custom of saying "Christ is Risen" before knocking a hardboiled painted egg against that of an opponent, who responds with "Truly He is Risen!" The one whose egg doesn't crack wins. In the Serbian town of Mokrin, people even compete in the "Egg-tapping World Cup." Ultimately, the egg is an enduring symbol of the Tomb that could not contain the Life bursting forth from within.

EASTER EGG HUNTS

Easter egg hunts are another popular activity. The joy children experience in finding real or candy-filled eggs reminds us of the joy the myrrh-bearing women experienced upon finding the empty tomb. Some communities (especially in Moldova, Ukraine, and Russia) have egg hunts among the decorated graves of cemeteries. This custom illustrates our belief that death can no longer destroy the bonds of love between us. As Saint Paul says, "I do not want you to be ignorant, brethren, concerning those who have fallen asleep, lest you sorrow as others who have no hope. For if we believe that Jesus died and rose again, even so God will bring with Him those who sleep in Jesus" (1 Thess. 4:13–14).

OLD TESTAMENT CONNECTION

After His Resurrection, Jesus explains to His apostles how He is the fulfillment of the words "which were written in the Law of Moses and the Prophets and the Psalms" (Luke 24:44). While Passover was the defining event of the Old Testament, it was ultimately a foreshadowing of Pascha (the Greek word for Passover), the defining event of the New (and everlasting) Testament.

FROM JEWISH PASSOVER TO CHRISTIAN PASCHA

1. The Passover lamb had no blemish.
1. Christ, the Lamb of God, has no sin.

2. No bones of the Passover lamb were broken.
2. No bones of Christ are broken.

3. The lamb's blood spared the firstborn sons of the Hebrews from physical death.
3. Christ's blood spares all of humanity from eternal death.

4. The Hebrews escaped physical slavery by passing over from Egypt to freedom through the Red Sea.
4. Christ frees us from spiritual slavery by passing us over from death to eternal life through His Cross.

If any man be devout and love God, let him enjoy this fair and radiant triumphal feast. If any man be a wise servant, let him rejoicing enter into the joy of his Lord. If any have labored long in fasting, let him now receive his recompense. If any have wrought from the first hour, let him today receive his just reward. If any have come at the third hour, let him with thankfulness keep the feast. If any have arrived at the sixth hour, let him have no misgivings; because he shall in nowise be deprived thereof. If any have delayed until the ninth hour, let him draw near, fearing nothing. If any have tarried even until the eleventh hour, let him, also, be not alarmed at his tardiness; for the Lord, who is jealous of his honor, will accept the last even as the first; he gives rest unto him who comes at the eleventh hour, even as unto him who has wrought from the first hour.

And he shows mercy upon the last, and cares for the first; and to the one he gives, and upon the other he bestows gifts. And he both accepts the deeds, and welcomes the intention, and honors the acts, and praises the offering. Wherefore, enter you all into the joy of your Lord; and receive your reward, both the first, and likewise the second. You rich and poor together, hold high the festival. You sober and you heedless, honor the day. Rejoice today, both you who have fasted and you who have

continued on page 44

continued from page 43

disregarded the fast. The table is full-laden; feast ye all sumptuously. The calf is fatted; let no one go hungry away.

Enjoy ye all the feast of faith: Receive ye all the riches of loving-kindness. Let no one bewail his poverty, for the universal kingdom has been revealed. Let no one weep for his iniquities, for pardon has shone forth from the grave. Let no one fear death, for the Savior's death has set us free. He that was held prisoner of it has annihilated it. By descending into Hell, He made Hell captive. He embittered it when it tasted of His flesh. And Isaiah, foretelling this, did cry: Hell, said he, was embittered, when it encountered Thee in the lower regions. It was embittered, for it was abolished. It was embittered, for it was mocked. It was embittered, for it was slain. It was embittered, for it was overthrown. It was embittered, for it was fettered in chains. It took a body, and met God face to face. It took earth, and encountered Heaven. It took that which was seen, and fell upon the unseen.

O Death, where is your sting? O Hell, where is your victory? Christ is risen, and you are overthrown. Christ is risen, and the demons are fallen. Christ is risen, and the angels rejoice. Christ is risen, and life reigns. Christ is risen, and not one dead remains in the grave. For Christ, being risen from the dead, is become the first fruits of those who have fallen asleep. To Him be glory and dominion unto ages of ages. Amen.

—Saint John Chrysostom

YESTERDAY I WAS CRUCIFIED WITH HIM;
TODAY I AM GLORIFIED WITH HIM.

YESTERDAY I DIED WITH HIM;
TODAY I AM MADE ALIVE WITH HIM.

YESTERDAY I WAS BURIED WITH HIM;
TODAY I AM RAISED UP WITH HIM.

ST. GREGORY THE THEOLOGIAN

FESTAL HYMNS

TROPARION: Christ is risen from the dead, trampling down death by death, and upon those in the tombs bestowing life!

KONTAKION: You descended into the tomb, O Immortal One; You destroyed the power of death! In victory You arose, O Christ our God, proclaiming "Rejoice" to the myrrh-bearing women, granting peace to Your apostles, and bestowing resurrection on the fallen.

FIRST ODE OF THE PASCHAL CANON: It is the day of resurrection! Let us be illumined for the feast! Pascha, the Pascha of the Lord! From death unto life, and from earth unto heaven has Christ our God led us, singing the song of victory: Christ is risen from the dead!

HYPAKOE: Before the dawn, Mary and the women came and found the stone rolled away from the tomb. They heard the angelic voice, "Why do you seek among the dead as a man the One who is Everlasting Light? Behold the clothes in the grave! Go and proclaim to the world: The Lord is risen! He has slain death, as He is the Son of God, saving the race of men."

PASCHAL HYMN TO THE THEOTOKOS: The angel cried to the Lady full of Grace: Rejoice, O pure Virgin! Again I say, Rejoice! Your Son is risen from His three days in the tomb! With Himself He has raised all the dead! Rejoice, all you people!

Shine! Shine! O New Jerusalem! The Glory of the Lord has shone on you! Exalt now and be glad, O Zion! Be radiant, O pure Theotokos, in the Resurrection of your Son!

THINK ABOUT IT . . .

"Do not be afraid; I am the First and the Last. I am He who lives, and was dead, and behold, I am alive forevermore. Amen. And I have the keys of Hades and of Death." (Rev. 1:17–18)

Every Sunday is the day of Resurrection. During Matins (Orthros) and the Divine Liturgy we sing hymns celebrating Christ's triumph over death. "When You, the Deathless Life, went down to death, You slew Hades by the lightning flash of Your divinity. And when You raised the dead from the lower world, all the Powers of Heaven cried aloud: Christ our God, Giver of life, glory to You" (Sunday troparion). Every Sunday, God grants us the opportunity to experience the divine triumph that took place 2000 years ago yet affects everyone and everything before and since. Every Sunday, God gives us the choice to take part in this eternal mystery, to let Him enter into our hearts and lift us up into the light of the endless day of His Resurrection. There is nothing to be afraid of any more; our souls and bodies are now in Christ's hands forever.

WHERE ARE YOU?

Pascha is the highlight of our liturgical year, the feast so great that without it the twelve feasts would lose their light and meaning. No matter where any of us find ourselves, there is nothing to fear now. "The Light has shone forth, awakening those who sleep in darkness and turning tears into joy." All we have to do is reach out, and Christ will pull us into His everlasting glory.

1 JESUS THE MESSIAH, through the Church gathered below Him, will forever remain the source of all good things (indicated by His blessing hand) and wisdom (indicated by the scroll in His other hand). Rising in the glorious circle of His mandorla, He is depicted in a way that resembles icons of the Last Judgment since "He is coming with clouds, and every eye will see Him, even they who pierced Him" (Rev. 1:7).

2 MARY THE THEOTOKOS—the temple of the incarnate God—personifies the Church, waiting for the return of her Christ. The icons show her standing between the angels, directly below Christ,

with a calm, anchoring stability. This depiction of her with hands stretched out in prayer resembles the Virgin of the Sign icons, which show the Christ-child in a heavenly circle within His mother, bringing divinity to humanity. With this connection in mind, it now looks as if Jesus has risen straight up from His mother and into the sky, bringing humanity to divinity.

3 THE HOLY ANGELS in the upper portion of the icon glorify Christ as He rises to heaven. The angels on earth gesture upward, reminding the apostles that Christ will return from heaven in a similar manner.

4 THE HOLY APOSTLES, having not yet received the Holy Spirit, are shown without halos. Some gaze up at Christ, while the rest look at Mary, the angels, or each other, expressing their amazement at Christ's Ascension. This is also a way of showing the varying stages of their spiritual lives.

5 SAINT PAUL, among others, is often shown with the disciples even though he wasn't present at the Ascension. All members of Christ's Church, no matter how far removed by time and space, are part of this elevation of human nature into the realm of the Divine.

THE ASCENSION OF CHRIST

For forty days, since Pascha, Christ has been appearing to His disciples, eating with them, showing them His wounds, testifying to the accomplishment of His Crucifixion and proving the reality of His Resurrection. Now they stand watching as the Son of God ascends, raising earth up to meet heaven.

"You shall receive power when the Holy Spirit has come upon you; and you shall be witnesses to Me in Jerusalem, and in all Judea and Samaria, and to the end of the earth" (Acts 1:8). These were Christ's last words to His apostles in Bethany. Then, as He lifted up His hands to bless them, He Himself was lifted up "and a cloud received Him out of their sight" (Acts 1:9). The apostles' response was to worship Him as God (Luke 24:52). As they kept their eyes raised to heaven, two angels appeared to tell them Christ would return in the same manner. The apostles were to follow His instructions and wait to receive the Holy Spirit in Jerusalem. Then they would be ready to "preach the gospel to every creature" (Mark 16:15) and show the world that the right hand of the Father, and not the grave, is where every human being belongs.

During their last conversation with Christ, the apostles ask if He is about to restore Israel as an earthly kingdom (Acts 1:6–7). Even after the Resurrection, they're still unable to see that Christ's love reaches beyond the boundaries of their nation. This is why we all need Pentecost. With humanity's cooperation, the Holy Spirit replaces confusion with clarity, foolishness with wisdom, and fear with love for all people as we struggle to fulfill His mission to make disciples of all nations.

Food for the Hungry

GOSPEL: LUKE 24:36–53

Now as they said these things, Jesus Himself stood in the midst of them, and said to them, "Peace to you." But they were terrified and frightened, and supposed they had seen a spirit. And He said to them, "Why are you troubled? And why do doubts arise in your hearts? Behold My hands and My feet, that it is I Myself. Handle Me and see, for a spirit does not have flesh and bones as you see I have."

When He had said this, He showed them His hands and His feet. But while they still did not believe for joy, and marveled, He said to them, "Have you any food here?" So they gave Him a piece of a broiled fish and some honeycomb. And He took it and ate in their presence.

Then He said to them, "These are the words which I spoke to you while I was still with you, that all things must be fulfilled which were written in the Law of Moses and the Prophets and the Psalms concerning Me." And He opened their understanding, that they might comprehend the Scriptures.

Then He said to them, "Thus it is written, and thus it was necessary for the Christ to suffer and to rise from the dead the third day, and that repentance and remission of sins should be preached in His name to all nations, beginning at Jerusalem. And you are witnesses of these things. Behold, I send the Promise of My Father upon you; but tarry in the city of Jerusalem until you are endued with power from on high."

continued on page 48

continued from page 47

And He led them out as far as Bethany, and He lifted up His hands and blessed them. Now it came to pass, while He blessed them, that He was parted from them and carried up into heaven. And they worshiped Him, and returned to Jerusalem with great joy, and were continually in the temple praising and blessing God. Amen.

Readings for Vespers: Isaiah 2:2–3; 62:10—63:9; Zechariah 14:1, 4, 8–11

Reading for Matins: Mark 16:9–20
Epistle Reading: Acts 1:1–12
Gospel Reading: Luke 24:36–53

OLD TESTAMENT CONNECTION

Christ's Ascension in the Psalms

He bowed the heavens also, and came down
With darkness under His feet.
And He rode upon a cherub, and flew;
He flew upon the wings of the wind.
(Psalm 18:9–10)

Who may ascend into the hill of the Lord?
Or who may stand in His holy place?
(Psalm 24:3–4)

Lift up your heads, O you gates!
And be lifted up, you everlasting doors!
And the King of glory shall come in.
(Psalm 24:7–10)

God has gone up with a shout,
The Lord with the sound of a trumpet.
Sing praises to God, sing praises!
Sing praises to our King, sing praises!
(Psalm 47:5–6)

The Lord said to my Lord,
"Sit at My right hand,
Till I make Your enemies Your footstool."
(Psalm 110:1)

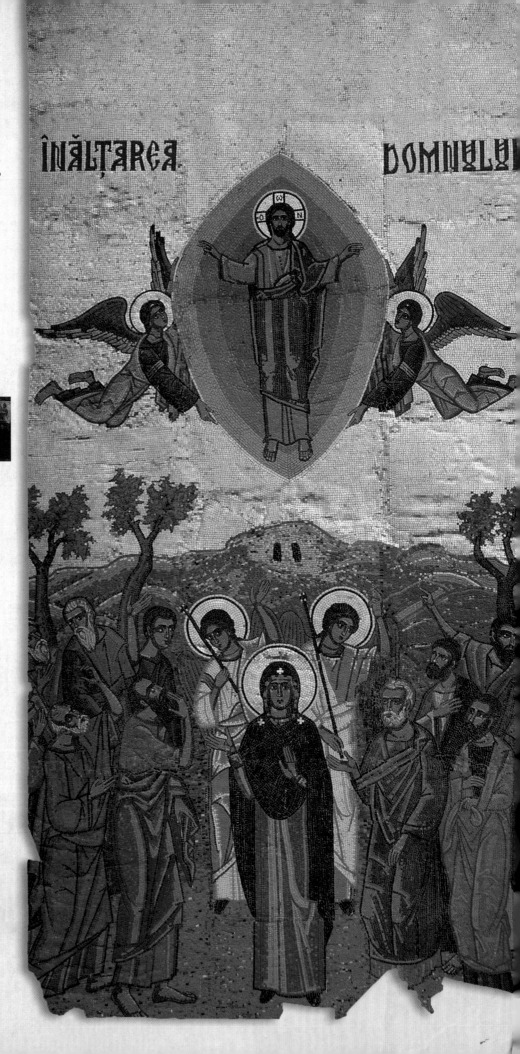

FESTAL HYMNS

TROPARION: You ascended in glory, O Christ our God, granting joy to Your disciples by the promise of the Holy Spirit. Through the blessing, they were assured that You are the Son of God, the Redeemer of the world!

KONTAKION: When you had fulfilled the dispensation for our sake, and united earth to heaven, You ascended in glory, O Christ our God, not being parted from those who love You, but remaining with them and crying, "I am with you and no one will be against you!"

ASCENSION CATHEDRAL
UNALASKA, ALASKA, USA

The first priest to serve this Aleutian island parish was Fr. John Veniaminov, now known to us as St. Innocent of Alaska. One of the two side chapels features an icon screen built by the saint himself. This chapel also houses the Gospel of Matthew that St. Innocent translated into Aleut.

Nevertheless, brethren, we must know that with Christ ascends neither pride, nor avarice, nor impurity; none of our vices will ascend with our Healer. So if we desire to ascend in company with Him, we must desist from sin and evil. We celebrate today the solemnity of the Ascension of the Lord. By celebrating this feast devoutly, virtuously, faithfully, piously, we ascend with Him and have our hearts above. For the resurrection of the Lord is our hope, and His ascension is our glorification.

—St. Augustine

THINK ABOUT IT

Our human nature now rises past the nine orders of angels to the throne of God, where He has always wanted us to be. Unfortunately, we've tried to "ascend" on our own terms—such as what happened with the Tower of Babel in the Old Testament. Christ now brings us up to "the right hand of the Father," so much higher than the builders at Babel could ever have imagined. This is why Jesus was lifted up on the Cross: to lift us into heaven. To enter into His glory, we too must rise above the ways of this world. "To him who overcomes I will grant to sit with Me on My throne, as I also overcame and sat down with My Father on His throne" (Rev. 3:21).

WHERE ARE YOU?

During the forty days of celebrating our risen Christ, we sometimes slide back into the harmful habits that we fought against during Lent. As Saint Paul reminds us, "If then you were raised with Christ, seek those things which are above, where Christ is, sitting at the right hand of God" (Col. 3:1). The gates of heaven are open, and God has prepared a place of honor for us. Let us not settle for anything less.

1 JESUS THE MESSIAH, the head of the Church, is physically not among the apostles anymore, as we can see by the empty seat of honor between Saints Peter and Paul. He has sent the Holy Spirit to guide and comfort us until the Second Coming. We who make up the Church are now His presence on earth.

2 THE HOLY SPIRIT is represented by the rays of light coming down from heaven to each of the apostles. Iconographers often substitute the apostles' halos with tongues of fire to indicate the presence of the Holy Spirit.

3 THE HOLY APOSTLES harmoniously face each other, displaying their oneness of mind and purpose. Their multicolored robes show that this unity doesn't mean the loss of diversity. Gospel writers like Matthew and Luke are often depicted holding the Gospels they will write, while the others hold scrolls that symbolize the teaching authority given to them by Christ. Their semicircular formation mirrors that of the darkened world—not to conform to it, but to transform it through the light of Christ.

4 PAUL, MARK, AND LUKE—who helped spread the gospel but were not present at Pentecost—are often included since this icon represents not only the earthly Church's beginning, but the divinely guided life of the Church throughout time.

5 THE COSMOS, the old kingly figure beneath the feet of the apostles, represents creation and the people, kingdoms, and authorities of the world. He stands in darkness because he hasn't yet received the light of Christ. His crown of worldly glory symbolizes the sins that ruled over humanity before Christ, while his old age reminds us that everything of this world falls victim to time and decay.

6 TWELVE SCROLLS, one for each apostle, lie on the cloth stretched between the Cosmos's hands, containing the message of the gospel. Through the gospel the Holy Spirit reaches out to the darkest corners of humanity, bringing light and life.

HOLY PENTECOST

Rushing wind, loud preaching in strange languages, accusations of wine-drinking—the descent of the Holy Spirit brings much excitement to those gathered for the Feast of Pentecost. Since it's through this heavenly outpouring that the world learns that God is Father, Son, and Holy Spirit, Pentecost is also the feast day of the Holy Trinity.

Ten days after Christ's Ascension, His followers gathered in Jerusalem to celebrate the Old Testament Pentecost, which recalled God's giving of the Law (including the Ten Commandments) to His people. The apostles had remained together in obedience to Christ's instructions to wait for the coming of the Holy Spirit. Yet they weren't prepared for the strong and sudden wind that rushed through the building. With this wind came the tongues of fire that appeared over their heads. Through this descent of the Holy Spirit, they could now speak languages they hadn't known before. They preached with newfound bravery, eloquence, and wisdom, leading three thousand people to repentance and baptism that very day. Heaven's gates opened up to all people, to "every nation under heaven" (Acts 2:5). The local language of each land had now become the sacred language of God.

The ancient foolishness of the builders of Babel is now undone by the descending wisdom of the Holy Spirit. Since the unifying love of God overshadows the pride and ambition of men, language and ethnicity are no longer barriers. Together, millions of people of diverse backgrounds make up the Church, the deified Body of Christ. Our calling is to mirror the divine unity that flows between the three Persons of the One God, who invites us all into His endless circle of love.

Food for the Hungry

ACTS 2:1–11

When the Day of Pentecost had fully come, they were all with one accord in one place. And suddenly there came a sound from heaven, as of a rushing mighty wind, and it filled the whole house where they were sitting. Then there appeared to them divided tongues, as of fire, and one sat upon each of them. And they were all filled with the Holy Spirit and began to speak with other tongues, as the Spirit gave them utterance. And there were dwelling in Jerusalem Jews, devout men, from every nation under heaven. And when this sound occurred, the multitude came together, and were confused, because everyone heard them speak in his own language. Then they were all amazed and marveled, saying to one another, "Look, are not all these who speak Galileans? And how is it that we hear, each in our own language in which we were born? Parthians and Medes and Elamites, those dwelling in Mesopotamia, Judea and Cappadocia, Pontus and Asia, Phrygia and Pamphylia, Egypt and the parts of Libya adjoining Cyrene, visitors from Rome, both Jews and proselytes, Cretans and Arabs—we hear them speaking in our own tongues the wonderful works of God."

Readings for Vespers: Numbers 11:16–17, 24–29; Joel 2:23–32; Ezekiel 36:24–28

Reading for Matins: John 20:19–23 • **Epistle Reading:** Acts 2:1–11 • **Gospel Reading:** John 7:37–52; 8:12
Epistle Reading for Monday of the Holy Spirit: Ephesians 5:8–19 • **Gospel Reading for Monday of the Holy Spirit:** Matthew 18:10–20

Clearly you are an epistle of Christ, ministered by us, written not with ink but by the Spirit of the living God, not on tablets of stone but on tablets of flesh, that is, of the heart. (2 Corinthians 3:3)

OLD TESTAMENT: SHAVUOT
(Hebrew word meaning *Festival of Weeks*)

1. Celebrated on the fiftieth day after Passover
2. Celebrated God's giving of the Law to Moses on Mt. Sinai
3. Reception of the Law led to the death of three thousand (Ex. 32:28)
4. Law was etched on tablets of stone
5. First fruits of the harvest were offered up to God

NEW TESTAMENT: PENTECOST
(Greek word meaning *Fiftieth*)

1. Celebrated on the fiftieth day after Pascha
2. Celebrates God's giving of the Holy Spirit to His followers on Mt. Zion (Jerusalem)
3. Reception of the Spirit led to the rebirth (baptism) of three thousand (Acts 2:41)
4. Law is now etched on "tablets of human hearts" (2 Cor. 3:3)
5. First fruits of Christ's harvest, the apostles, offer their lives to God

Master, Lord of all, our God and Redeemer, the hope of all, at the ends of the earth and far away at sea, on this latter great and saving day of Pentecost You disclosed to us the mystery of the holy, consubstantial, co-eternal, and life-giving Trinity, indivisible yet distinct, and in the descent and presence of Your holy and life-giving Spirit poured out its grace upon Your holy Apostles in the form of fiery tongues, making them proclaimers and confessors of our holy Faith, of true knowledge of God.

— St. Basil the Great, from the Third Kneeling Prayer of Pentecost Vespers*

*The kneeling prayers mark the first time since Pascha that we penitentially kneel and make prostrations as we ask God to make us worthy of receiving the Holy Spirit.

festal tradition
Pentecost and Plants

According to Jewish tradition, flowers blossomed on Mount Sinai when God gave His people the Law (the Torah), which includes the first five books of the Bible. Jewish communities commemorate this event during Shavuot—the Hebrew word for Pentecost—by adorning their synagogues and homes with greenery and flowers. This complements the Jewish notion that Moses was like a matchmaker who brought together Israel (the bride) and God (the groom). The Torah served as the wedding contract, while the cloud covering Sinai was seen as the wedding canopy. Furthermore, Shavuot was a joyful harvest festival, during which the Jews brought the first fruits to the temple (Ex. 23:16).

To this day there exists a beautiful connection between the Jewish celebration of Shavuot and the Church's celebration of Pentecost. In some traditions, parishioners lovingly decorate the sacred spaces of their churches with flowers, fruits, vegetables, and even potted trees from their homes. The plants remind us that Christ's Bride—the Church—will always be alive and vibrant since she is united with the Source of Life. Pentecost is the gift Jesus gives to His bride. We've received something even greater than the Law; we've received the grace of the Spirit of God. Now we are called to be faithful to our Bridegroom. As St. Paul says, "It is no longer I who live, but Christ lives in me; and the life which I now live in the flesh I live by faith in the Son of God, who loved me and gave Himself for me" (Gal. 2:20).

Post-Communion hymn from the Liturgy of St. John Chrysostom

We have seen the True Light! We have received the Heavenly Spirit! We have found the True Faith, worshiping the Undivided Trinity, who has saved us.

HOLY TRINITY MONASTERY
METEORA, GREECE

Meteora means "suspended in the air," which is a fitting way to describe the Greek monasteries built on the tops of rock columns. Accessed by a narrow stairway, Holy Trinity is the most difficult to reach. Before the steps were built, visitors were pulled up by nets that were only replaced after "the Lord let them break."

METEORA

FESTAL HYMNS

TROPARION: Blessed are You, O Christ our God! You have revealed the fishermen as most wise by sending down upon them the Holy Spirit; through them You drew the world into Your net. O Lover of Man, glory to You!

KONTAKION: When the Most High came down and confused the tongues, He divided the nations; but when He distributed the tongues of fire, He called all to unity. Therefore, with one voice, we glorify the all-Holy Spirit!

THINK ABOUT IT . . .

Christ's parable of the mustard seed (Matt. 13:31–32) can be applied to the Descent of the Holy Spirit on Pentecost. The apostles, the small group of fishermen who are as "insignificant" as mustard seeds, will change the whole world. While John baptized with water, they are now "baptized with the Holy Spirit" (Acts 1:5). The seed of faith planted by Christ is "watered" by the third Person of the Holy Trinity. To this day the Church continues to spread across the earth, offering shelter from spiritual predators. The Church welcomes all people, all "the birds of the air," to "come and nest in its branches."

WHERE ARE YOU?

From the Nativity of the Theotokos to the Ascension of Christ—the feasts have connected us to the reality that God has connected Himself to us. Pentecost celebrates the culmination of the gift of His Incarnation, the sending of God Himself to dwell in His Church, in His people. Through the Holy Spirit, we are now Christ's presence on earth. This is the world's new beginning. Through the Church, humanity can return to paradise.

❶ JESUS THE MESSIAH radiates with humanity's original beauty, the beauty that once again will belong to the righteous in the age to come. His divinity, represented by the blue mandorla, shines through His humanity—as it always has. On Tabor, He's allowed His disciples to see as much of it as they can bear.

❷ GOD THE FATHER is invisibly present. Once again He calls Jesus His beloved Son, connecting this feast to Theophany, the first revelation of the Holy Trinity.

❸ THE HOLY SPIRIT, the luminous cloud that that covers the mountaintop, is represented by the geometrical figure in Christ's mandorla.

❹ ELIJAH THE PROPHET, at the Savior's right hand—the spot where John the Baptist stands in the Theophony icon—represents all the prophets, whose words ultimately point to Jesus Christ. Having been taken up into the heavenly realm by a fiery chariot, he also represents the living.

❺ MOSES THE LAWGIVER holds the book of the Law, which Christ fulfills perfectly. Having died before reaching the Promised Land, he represents the dead.

❻ PETER THE CHIEF APOSTLE represents Faith since, just days before the Transfiguration, he was the first to confess Jesus as "the Christ, the Son of the Living God." His hand gestures toward Jesus, indicating that he is saying, "Lord, it is good for us to be here" (Matt. 17:4).

❼ JOHN THE THEOLOGIAN, who will stay with Jesus during the Crucifixion, represents Love. Christ's youngest apostle—as indicated by the lack of a beard—he is always shown in the middle, directly below the feet of Christ.

❽ JAMES THE SON OF THUNDER, John's older brother, represents Hope since his strong belief in the Kingdom of Heaven led him to become the first of the twelve disciples to be martyred. He lies on his back covering his eyes—he has been knocked off his feet by Christ's dazzling glory.

THE TRANSFIGURATION OF CHRIST
August 6

His face radiating like the sun, His clothes shining with the uncreated light of God, Jesus stands transfigured (changed in appearance) before His disciples on Mount Tabor. He has opened their eyes to see His ever-present divine glory.

After predicting His approaching Crucifixion, Jesus led Peter, James, and John (the same three disciples who would witness His agony in Gethsemane) up Mount Tabor. At the summit He was transfigured before them, shining with bright, heavenly light. Moses and Elijah, who both had mountaintop encounters with God in the Old Testament era, were also miraculously present. Peter, wanting to honor them along with Jesus and to remain caught up in this glory, suggested putting up booths for them, since it was the Feast of Tabernacles. At this point, the luminous cloud of the Holy Spirit descended, and the voice of the Father said, "This is My beloved Son. Hear Him!" (Mark 9:7). The three apostles fell on their faces in awe. Jesus went down and comforted them with a reassuring touch, saying, "Arise, and do not be afraid" (Matt. 17:7). Lifting their heads, they saw that they were alone again with Christ, who instructed them, "Tell the vision to no one until the Son of man is risen from the dead" (Matt. 17:9).

On Tabor, Moses and Elijah speak to Jesus about His coming "exodus" (according to the original Greek of Luke's Gospel) in Jerusalem. This reference connects the Crucifixion (freeing us from the bondage to sin and death) to Moses' leading of Israel on its forty-year journey out of bondage in Egypt. Fittingly, forty days after the Feast of the Transfiguration we have the Feast of the Exaltation of the Holy Cross, a day when we celebrate the instrument of our freedom.

Food for the Hungry

THE GOSPEL OF MATTHEW 17:1–9

Now after six days Jesus took Peter, James, and John his brother, and led them up on a high mountain by themselves; and He was transfigured before them. His face shone like the sun, and His clothes became as white as the light.
And behold, Moses and Elijah appeared to them, talking with Him. Then Peter answered and said to Jesus, "Lord, it is good for us to be here; if You wish, let us make here three tabernacles: one for You, one for Moses, and one for Elijah."

While he was still speaking, behold, a bright cloud overshadowed them; and suddenly a voice came out of the cloud, saying, "This is My beloved Son, in whom I am well pleased. Hear Him!" And when the disciples heard it, they fell on their faces and were greatly afraid. But Jesus came and touched them and said, "Arise, and do not be afraid."
When they had lifted up their eyes, they saw no one but Jesus only.

Now as they came down from the mountain, Jesus commanded them, saying,
"Tell the vision to no one until the Son of Man is risen from the dead."

Readings for Vespers: Exodus 24:12–18; 33:11–23; 34:4–6, 8; 1 Kings 19:3–9, 11–13, 15–16

Reading for Matins: Luke 9:28–36 • **Epistle Reading:** 2 Peter 1:10–19 • **Gospel Reading:** Matthew 17:1–9 • **Additional Reading:** Mark 9:1–8

OLD TESTAMENT CONNECTION

In the past Christ led Israel in the wilderness with the pillar of fire and the cloud; and today ineffably He has shone forth in light upon Mount Tabor.
(Matins, Canticle 3, First Canon)

ELIJAH

1. Represents the Prophets
2. Encountered God on Mt. Carmel
3. Taken up to heaven in a fiery chariot while still living

MOSES

1. Represents the Law
2. Encountered God on Mt. Sinai
3. Died before reaching the Promised Land

JESUS

1. The fulfillment of the Law and the Prophets
2. Is the God encountered by Moses and Elijah
3. Is the God of the living and the dead

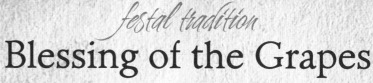

festal tradition
Blessing of the Grapes

The tradition of bringing grapes and other fruits to be blessed in church on the Feast of the Transfiguration has deep roots. The people of Israel had a harvest celebration called the Festival of the Booths, a reminder of their time spent wandering in the desert. As they made their way to the Promised Land, they lived in tents like the ones Peter wanted to put up on Tabor. The festival later became linked to the anticipated future, when God would dwell with His people. The Church, the New Israel, celebrates the Transfiguration as the fulfillment of this blessed state. Jesus, now revealed as both divine and human, unites us with God in a way Israel could never have imagined. The Transfiguration also calls us to look forward to Christ's Second Coming, when all of nature's original beauty will be restored. Believers bring grapes to church to be blessed and shared as a sign of this final transfiguration of everything. Grapes are a perfect symbol, growing and changing colors as they ripen in the light. Also, in a beautiful series of gift exchanges between God and His people, certain grapes are turned into wine and offered to Him; then this wine, along with the altar bread, is turned into His Body and Blood and offered back to us. In the Eucharist, the fruits of nature have become God. The Gospel proclaims that this kind of transfiguration is our destiny as well: "Then the righteous will shine forth as the sun in the kingdom of their Father" (Matthew 13:43).

FESTAL HYMNS

TROPARION: You were transfigured on the mountain, O Christ God, revealing Your glory to Your disciples as far as they could bear it. Let Your everlasting Light also shine upon us sinners, through the prayers of the Theotokos. O Giver of Light, glory to You!

KONTAKION: On the Mountain You were Transfigured, O Christ God, and Your disciples beheld Your glory as far as they could see it, so that when they would behold You crucified, they would understand that Your suffering was voluntary, and would proclaim to the world that You are truly the Radiance of the Father!

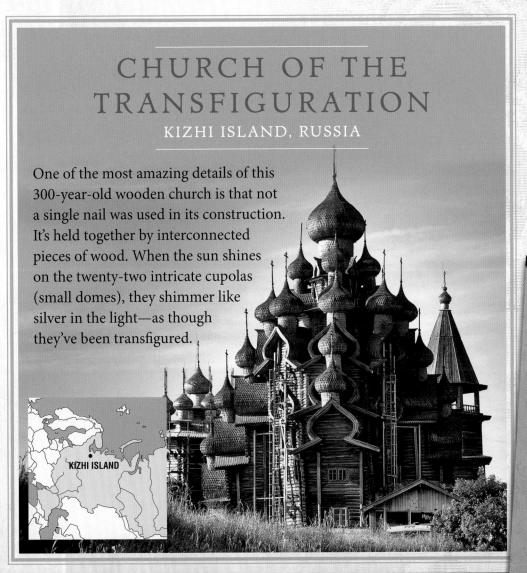

CHURCH OF THE TRANSFIGURATION
KIZHI ISLAND, RUSSIA

One of the most amazing details of this 300-year-old wooden church is that not a single nail was used in its construction. It's held together by interconnected pieces of wood. When the sun shines on the twenty-two intricate cupolas (small domes), they shimmer like silver in the light—as though they've been transfigured.

KIZHI ISLAND

Through the Fall our nature was stripped of divine illumination and resplendence. But the Logos of God had pity upon our disfigurement, and in His compassion He took our nature upon Himself, and on Tabor He manifested it to His elect disciples clothed once again most brilliantly. As St. John Chrysostom says, He shows what we once were and what we shall become through Him in the age to come, if we choose to live our present life as far as possible in accordance with His ways.
—St. Gregory Palamas

THINK ABOUT IT . . .

Even Christ's clothing shines brightly, showing that everything and everyone connected to Him can shine with His Light. In fact, this is our calling: to shine with heavenly beauty in a darkened world. Our examples, the saints, are like stained-glass windows. They align themselves with God and let His light shine through them. Saints who have shone with the Light of Tabor include Anthony, Symeon the New Theologian, Gregory Palamas, Seraphim of Sarov, and Elder Nektary of Optina, among many others. With them we look forward to the final transfiguration at the end of time, when we'll be so free from sin that we won't even remember what darkness is.

WHERE ARE YOU?

The liturgical year is almost over; how far up Tabor have we climbed? Sometimes we slip back down because we try to ascend without the cross to steady and support us. In icons of the Crucifixion, we often replace the sign's mocking words "The King of the Jews" with "The King of Glory." Jesus is as much the King of Glory on Golgotha as He is on Tabor, and He wants to share this glory with us.

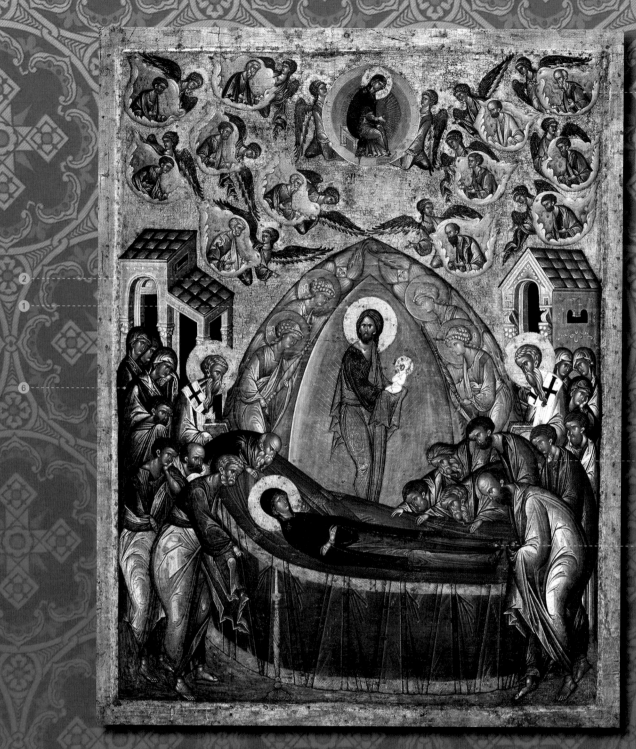

1 JESUS THE MESSIAH is at the heart of this icon, much as the Resurrection is at the heart of the Christian year and the Christian life. Union with Him, the Conqueror of Death, is the goal of our earthly struggle.

2 THE MANDORLA OF CHRIST shows His glorious divinity. It is so large that the red curtain that normally indicates a scene is taking place indoors is absent; there is no more "ceiling" between us and heaven. Christ has broken down all barriers; death can no longer dissolve the bond of love between those on earth and those in the afterlife.

3 THE THEOTOKOS's pure body lies in peace before her Son while her spotless soul rests in His hands. The way in which Christ is holding her soul, wrapped in swaddling clothes, reminds us of the icons in which Mary is holding her Child. Christ is now accepting Mary on behalf of heaven in the same way that she accepted Him on behalf of earth.

4 THE ANGELS, transporting the apostles from the ends of the earth to be with Mary, show us that heaven and earth are truly meeting. The Theotokos is also shown among the angels up at the top of the icon, since she now resides in the heavenly realm in both soul and body.

5 PETER, PAUL, AND THE OTHER APOSTLES have assembled to honor Mary, the "gate" through which salvation has come into the world. Since her Son has destroyed the barrier caused by death, the apostles and all believers can continue asking for her prayers and intercession.

6 BISHOPS AND THE WOMEN OF JERUSALEM show that all, male and female, Jew and Gentile, gather around the Mother of our Hope and Life. The gates of heaven that have opened up for Mary are also open for all of humanity. The bishops represented in icons of the Dormition include some combination of the following: James-the brother of our Lord and first bishop of Jerusalem, Timothy-who was converted to Christ through Saint Paul, and Hierotheus and Dionysios—former pagans who became bishops of Athens.

THE DORMITION OF THE THEOTOKOS

The apostles have witnessed the perfect fulfillment of a life lived in Christ, so united to His that we honor Mary with lamentations like those offered to her Son on Holy Friday: "How can the tomb contain your body, which contained the One who cannot be contained?" If we follow her example, our souls can become like hers and find everlasting rest in Christ's hands.

According to ancient tradition, the apostles—who had been off preaching in faraway lands—were transported by angels to bid farewell to the dying mother of their Master. Only Thomas was not with them. At the time of her death, Christ came to escort His mother's soul to heaven. The apostles then led a procession to Mary's tomb in Gethsemane, where they buried her body. Three days later, Thomas arrived to offer a final earthly goodbye to the Mother of God. When the apostles opened the tomb and found it empty, they realized Christ had carried His mother's immaculate body up to heaven.

The Dormition is called the "summer Pascha" since it cultivates hope in our own personal Passover into eternal life. Mary—the new Eve, the new mother of humanity—shows us that the end of earthly life has become a passage to an ever-deepening union with her Son. If we follow her example, then we too will become citizens of paradise, never again to fall. This is why we journey through the feasts year after year, stumbling often but never giving up as we seek to be one with the God who became one of us.

Food for the Hungry

APOCRYPHAL BOOK OF ST. JOHN THE THEOLOGIAN*

The apostles said all these things to the holy mother of God, why they had come, and in what way; and she stretched her hands to heaven and prayed, saying: I adore, and praise, and glorify Your much to be praised name, O Lord, because You have looked upon the lowliness of Your handmaiden, and because You that are mighty have done great things for me; and, behold, all generations shall count me blessed. And after the prayer she said to the apostles: Cast incense, and pray. And when they had prayed, there was thunder from heaven, and there came a fearful voice, as if of chariots; and, behold, a multitude of a host of angels and powers, and a voice, as if of the Son of man, was heard, and the seraphim in a circle round the house where the holy, spotless mother of God and virgin was lying, so that all who were in Bethlehem beheld all the wonderful things, and came to Jerusalem and reported all the wonderful things that had come to pass.

Readings for Vespers: Genesis 28:10–17; Ezekiel 43:27—44:4; Proverbs 9:1–11

Reading for Matins: Luke 1:39–49, 56 • **Epistle Reading:** Philippians 2:5–11 • **Gospel Reading:** Luke 10:38–42; 11:27–28

*The Church affirms that while this book contains errors and inaccuracies, it also contains accounts and information that are edifying and true.

OLD TESTAMENT CONNECTION: MARY, THE CHILD OF GOD

EVE

- Listened to the voice of Satan
- Granted herself access to the fruit of the tree of knowledge of good and evil
- Her flesh was taken from Adam
- Brought corruption and death into the world
- Her disobedience led to living death
- Body taken by the grave; soul taken by Hades
- Body decayed in the earth

MARY

- Listened to the voice of God
- Submitted to God's will and became the dwelling place of the Wisdom of God
- Gave her flesh to the Son of God
- Brought salvation and life into the world
- Her obedience led to death-defying life
- Body and soul taken into heaven
- Body experienced no corruption

DORMITION CATHEDRAL IN THE MONASTERY OF THE KIEV CAVES
KIEV, UKRAINE

Bombed during World War II, this church was recently restored as the jewel of the monastery, also known as the Pecherskaya Lavra. This huge monastery, nearly a thousand years old, is composed of an intricate complex of catacombs and underground churches and cells, in which the monks took refuge during the Tatar invasions.

KIEV
UKRAINE

festal tradition
The Snakes of Cephalonia

The unique aspect of this tradition is that it's kept by snakes. Each year on the Greek island of Cephalonia, a group of European cat snakes makes an apparent pilgrimage to the Church of the Dormition soon after the Feast of the Transfiguration. This has been going on since the 1700s in the village of Markopoulo. The snakes come out of a bell tower that was part of a convent destroyed by the Ottoman Turks in 1705 and crawl over and around the icons of the Theotokos until the Feast of the Dormition.

The link between the Transfiguration and the Dormition points to the Theotokos as one whose life has been so transformed by Christ that death is no longer something to fear. The small snakes themselves are symbols of this blessed state of being. They are venomous, but due to the position of their fangs, they can't deliver their venom to humans. They are completely docile, showing no malicious inclination toward people. In fact, they have, from time to time, been credited as miraculous sources of healing. Death has truly lost its sting! The curse is abolished, and there is no more enmity between the serpent and the New Eve. The relationship has been restored in the same way humanity's relationship to God has been restored.

For the true Christian there is no death. Death was conquered by Christ on the cross. But there is a translation, i.e., a rearrangement of his condition, i.e. his soul is in another place, in another age, in another world beyond the grave, eternal, without end; that is what is meant by "falling asleep." It is as if it were a temporary dream after which, by the voice of the Lord and the fearful yet wonderful trumpet of the Archangel, all the dead shall live and come forth each to his place: either to the resurrection of life or to the resurrection of condemnation (John 5:29).
—Saint John of Kronstadt

FESTAL HYMNS

TROPARION: In giving birth you preserved your virginity. In falling asleep you did not forsake the world, O Theotokos! You were translated to life, O Mother of Life, and by your prayers you deliver our souls from death.

KONTAKION: Neither the tomb nor death could hold the Theotokos, who is constant in prayer and our firm hope in her intercessions. For being the Mother of Life, she was translated to life by the One who dwelt in her virginal womb.

THINK ABOUT IT . . .

When our earthly life comes to its end, we don't want to leave this world—like an infant reluctant to leave the cozy warmth and darkness of its mother's womb. But in the same way that an infant couldn't possibly fathom the life and beauty in the world outside the womb, we can't possibly fathom the unending joy and light of heaven. We refer to death as a "falling asleep" because we close our eyes in this world, then open them in the endless day of the next, when we find ourselves in Christ's arms forever.

WHERE ARE YOU?

The cycle of church feasts begins and ends with the Theotokos, our greatest example of one who has been saved by Christ. Heaven has met earth; now salvation is ours to have. The angels rejoice as they witness us rising up past the clutches of the enemy and into the endless day of the Resurrection. Each year, our spiritual journey around this circle of feasts is meant to bring us closer to the One who is at its center, the One who calls us to let His light shine through our being in an endless day of brightness and joy.

CALENDAR OF THE GREAT FEASTS AND FASTS OF THE CHURCH

THE TWELVE GREAT FEASTS

Dates are given in Gregorian followed by Julian calendar.

FIXED FEASTS

The Nativity of the Theotokos
September 8/21

The Elevation of the Cross
September 14/27

The Entrance of the Theotokos
November 21/December 4

The Nativity of Christ
December 25/January 7

The Theophany of Christ
January 6/19

The Meeting of the Lord in the Temple
February 2/15

The Annunciation to the Theotokos
March 25/April 7

The Transfiguration of Christ
August 6/19

The Dormition of the Theotokos
August 15/28

MOVABLE FEASTS

(depending on the date of Pascha)

Palm Sunday
The Sunday before Pascha

Ascension Thursday
Forty days after Pascha

Pentecost Sunday
Fifty days after Pascha

Divine Liturgy is celebrated every Sunday throughout the calendar year.

The following are some other feasts that are often celebrated with a Divine Liturgy:

Beginning of the Church Year
September 1/14

The Protection of the Theotokos
October 1/14

Synaxis of the Archangels
November 8/21

The Feast of Saint Nektarios the Wonderworker
November 9/22

The Feast of Saint Nicholas of Myra
December 6/19

The Feast of Saint Steven the First Martyr
December 27/January 9

The Feast of Saint Basil the Great
January 1/14

The Circumcision of Our Lord
January 1/14

The Feast of Saint Anthony the Great
January 17/30

The Feast of the Three Hierarchs
January 30/February 12

The Feast of the Great Martyr George
April 23/May 6

The Feast of Saints Cyril and Methodius
May 11/24

The Feast of Saint John of Shanghai and San Francisco
June 19/July 2

The Nativity of Saint John the Baptist
June 24/July 7

The Feast of Saints Peter and Paul
June 29/July 12

The Feast of All Saints of North America
July 2/15

The Feast of the Prophet Elijah
July 20/August 2

The Feast of Saint Mary Magdalene
July 22/August 4

The Beheading of Saint John the Baptist
August 29/July 11

The patronal feast day of your parish

THE FASTS

Advent (40 days)
November 15–December 24
November 28–January 6

Great Lent and Holy Week
(7 weeks)
Clean Monday to Pascha

The Apostles' Fast (variable length)
Monday after All Saints' Day
(Sunday after Pentecost) until
the eve of the Feast of Ss. Peter
and Paul
June 29/July 12

The Dormition Fast (2 weeks)
August 1–14/14–27

INDIVIDUAL FASTING DAYS

The Great Feast of the Exaltation of the Cross
September 14/27

The Eve of the Theophany
January 5/18

The Beheading of St. John the Baptist
August 29/September 11

Wednesdays and Fridays
apart from:
Christmastide
December 25–January 4/
January 7–19

Variation:
Renewal Week
(the week after Pascha)
or
all of Eastertide
(Pascha–Ascension)

The week following the Sunday of the Publican and the Pharisee
(the third week before Great Lent)

Trinity Week (the week after Pentecost)

Fasting from meat only:
Cheese Week (the week before Great Lent)

Fish is permitted on Wednesdays and Fridays when they coincide with one of the Great Feasts (except for the Feast of the Exaltation of the Cross).

DATES OF ORTHODOX PASCHA AND LATIN EASTER

	ORTHODOX PASCHA	LATIN EASTER
2016	May 1	March 27
2017	April 16	April 16
2018	April 8	April 1
2019	April 28	April 21
2020	April 19	April 12
2021	May 2	April 4
2022	April 24	April 17
2023	April 16	April 9
2024	May 5	March 31
2025	April 20	April 20

IC XC

DONORS

A warm thanks from the Ancient Faith Publishing team to all those who helped make *Heaven Meets Earth* possible:

Matthew Ablan
In memory of all the victims of abortion
The Aldrich Clan
Kira/Kyriake for her daughter Anastasia
Stephen and Denise Anderson
Tatiana Kiaqaq Andrew
Annunciation Press
Holy Assumption Monastery
Assumption of the Blessed Virgin Mary Greek Orthodox Church,
    Long Beach, California
Frank Avant
St. Basil the Great Orthodox Mission, Marietta, Georgia
Constance Mary Beatty
In memory of Steve and Rose Bellows
Michael Berkshire
Connie Bille
In loving memory of Mary Bittenbinder
In memory of Dan Bjeletich
Lisa and Cody Bornejko
The Boskovski Family—Ace, Olga, Mile, Johnny, Steven, Christopher,
    and Nicholas
In memory of Jon Allen Boyer
Dn. Gary and Melissa Braun
Brigid
Jeff Brooks
On behalf of my mentor and friend who was an inspiration for seeking
    the true Church and Holy Orthodoxy, Fr. Dale Brown
The NH Brown Family
Michael Bryzak
Brian and Janel Burley
Silouan Burns and family
Mark Butt
Benjamin Cabe
Angela Doll Carlson
In memory of Kalia Carlson, may her memory be eternal
Carolyn Carmack
Cassimatis Family
Elene Catrakilis
Caty
Helena Cermakova
Cassandra Chamallas
Aaron and Terri Clayton
Costa and Maro
In honor of Rev. Fr. Paul Costopoulos
Thom and Christine Crowe
Fr. Andrew Stephen Damick
Chryss and Michael Danielek
On behalf of Carolyn, Rich, Harry and George Davis and Emilia Wenger
Keith and Embree Deason
Mary Dibs
Cheryl and David Doely
John Dounias
Sean P. Doyle
In memory of Sharon Drinkle
In memory of Gage Edwards
The Edwards Family
The Etchepare Family
V. Rev. John D. Finley

Forerunner Books and Nina Adams
On behalf of the Fortais and Pierpont Families
Jason Founts
Diana Fowler
In memory of Stamatis and Marianthi Frangeskaki
French
In memory of John Frimenko
Hayley Fulbright
Paul and Ramia Fuller
Anna Gage
Andreatta and Bruce Geerdes
Dottie Genatone
Saint George Greek Orthodox Church, Eugene,
    Oregon
Steve Georgiou
Melody A. Gesell
In memory of Fr. Peter Gillquist *(two donors)*
In memory of Rev. Fr. Soterios Gouvellis—
    Blessed Memory
Grace, Eve, and Annie
Nancy DeHaven Hall
Fr. Andrew Hanna
Troy & Carla Harris
In memory of Erena Haynes
In memory of my parents, Dean and Betty Helms
The Henderson Family
Jason Hess
On behalf of Holy Cross, Yakima, Washington
John Hudson
J Huff
Donald Hughes
Ken and Myrna Hull
Bill Humble
Ken Hutchins
Dr. and Mrs. Brian Jackson
In memory of Liljana and Slobodan Jankovic
On behalf of David and Geraldine Jennings
Simon Jennings
The Jensen Family
Reba Jinkins
In memory of my parents, Joan and Mort
In memory of Marianna Jodko *(two donors)*
St. John the Forerunner Orthodox Church,
    Indianapolis, Indiana
Stephen Johnson
To the grandchildren of Tom and Maye Johnson
Deacon Haralambos Joiner
Lee and Linda Joiner
The Jordan Family
The Josheff III Family
Steven Jug
In memory of Rev. Fr. Elias Kalariotes—
    Blessed Memory
Angela Kaplan
In memory of Yousef Karraz
In honor of Bethany, Adam, and Elaina Kaufman
Doug and Kristi King
The Kotinek Family
Donald H. Kraft
Ted Laliotis
Natallia Lambrecht
The Leclercq Family
In memory of Rev. Fr. Constantine Leftheris—
    Blessed Memory

Legacy Icons
In memory of Larry Letten
The Lewis Family
Michael and Sumi Lineback
On behalf of Logan
Mary Lou Longworth
Alan David Lovell
For our boys, Lucas, Anders, Amos, and Patrick
St. Luke Orthodox Anglican Church, Sikeston, Missouri
Lydia
Evan Lygeros
In memory of Jeremy Mains
The good health of my husband, Very Rev. George
    Manneh
Clifford John Manning
Maria
Douglas and Rose Marsh
Bryan E. Martin
On behalf of Francesca Martini
Aleks Matza
The McCallum Family
Marlene McCracken—in memory of Raymond, Jr.
In memory of Lynda Joanna McCroskery
Rev. Sister Susan Dean McReynolds, OCC
Valerie Melde
Samuel F. Messerschmidt
The Meyer Family
In memory of Sharon Lynne Michalski
The Mogish Family
Craig and Elaine Morfas
Bill and Josie Morrison
Diane and Ted Moshos
The Munaco Family
Nicholas Muzekari
Nicodemus
In memory of Nikolaos
Helen Norton
Miranda and Thomas Oberhausen
The O'Drudy Family (Leo, Tricia, Sean, and Nora)
Orthodox Church in America
VPSO Gerald OTTO
Frank Papafotiou
Fr. Vassilios Papavassiliou
In memory of Chris Pazeotopoulos
Daniel and Sara Catherine Pennington
The Peteya Family
Deacon Sean Petrisko
In honor of Father Peter and Khouria Pamela Pier
Dr. and Mrs. Michael A. Pikos
Fr. Barnabas Powell
Pascha Press
Carmen "Catherine" Pereira Pucilowski
Wendy Regas
In honor of the Ritz family
Elise Roberts
Perry and Nadina Robinson and Family
In memory of Fr. Andrew Sabak, Pani Anna,
    and Timothy Sabak
Nikolai Salamakha
Jean Sam
The Samara Family
In memory of Annie Saravolatz
The Schwengel Family
Brandon Scott-Omenka

The Segvich Family
Gail Shannon, in memory of Howard Shannon
The Shaws
For Shehadeh and Sofia
John and Sharon Shingara
Sider-Roses
In memory of Joseph and Alexandra Siffri
The Sill Family
In memory of Mr. and Mrs. Billy Drue Sipe
In memory of Ralph and Barbara Skalac
Kosmas & Stavroula Skinas
The Skowron Family
Father Dennis Smith
John and Nancy Smith
Joshua Smith
Norman Smith
In memory of Kevin Sparkman
The Speier Family
Columba Spence
Ryan D. G. Stout
Jason and Stacy Streit
Stephen and Maria
The Suehs Family
Philip and Artemis Tamoush
Donald J. Tamulonis Jr., MD
Justin Kia Lih Tan
Tatiana
In memory of Nathaniel S. Taylor
In memory of Theodore and Evangelia
In memory of our Parents—Thomas and Mae
Joyce Thomsen-Blake
Mary Tickel
For the health and salvation of Nicholas and
    Kathryn Tjoa, by their parents
In memory of Tom
Andrew and Daphni Tsongranis
Melanie and Marc Turgeon
The Twito Family
In memory of Helena VandenOever
In memory of Rev. Fr. Emanuel Vasilakis —
    Blessed Memory
Athena and Jerry Vasilatos
In memory of Rt. Rev. Mitred Archpriest
    Nikolajs Vieglais
In memory of Paul and Lola Vranas
The Vuckovic Family
Bob Vunovich
In memory of the Very Rev. Gordon Walker
Chad, Annette, and Kaylee Warkentin
James Weaver
The Weiss Family
Krista M. West
Susan, Jacquline, and Ravyn Williams
In memory of Fr. Thomas Williams
James Wilson
Mattie Windham
Laurie Woolworth and Family
Xenia Diane Mary
The Xenos Family
Judith Tabitha Yant
Yocepha from Ohio
Valerie Yova
and 96 other anonymous donors

OUR FAMILY FESTAL TRADITIONS